The Pretzel Cookbook

The Pretzel Cookbook

A NEW TWIST ON EVERYONE'S FAVORITE SNACK

Priscilla Warren

RUNNING PRESS
PHILADELPHIA · LONDON

9 8 7 6 5 4 3 2 1
Digit on the right indicates the number of this printing
Library of Congress Control Number: 2007938774
ISBN: 978-0-7624-3224-0

Cover and Interior design by Amanda Richmond
Edited by Diana C. von Glahn
Typography: Avenir, Bembo, and Gigglescript

This book may be ordered by mail from the publisher.
Please include $2.50 for postage and handling.
But try your bookstore first!

Running Press Book Publishers
2300 Chestnut Street
Philadelphia, PA 19103-4371

Visit us on the web!
www.runningpresscooks.com

To my mother Barbara, who is grace and faith personified. Your quiet dignity and love have kept my spirit buoyed and my heart happy. Koya and Tristan—who had to endure me as their "Auntie/Mommy" and came out relatively unscathed (you can pay for therapy later)—you are both intelligent, caring, talented human beings and I'm proud of you every day. Thank you for loving me back. And to the apple of my eye, my "grandson" Jeremiah, who is incredibly curious about the world and is the greatest joy in my life.

Contents

74 SAVORY FILLED PRETZELS

ACKNOWLEDGMENTS

There are many people who contributed to the final result of this cookbook. They know who they are, but I like to see some of their names in print. Here is my 'To Sir, with love' moment:

This book wouldn't be in your hands without the kind, patient, and very often befuddled (due to my ignorance) efforts of Diana von Glahn, my editor and dear friend. Her patience and generosity know no bounds (this is not a paid endorsement). She's got a quick mind, an even quicker wit, and I'm proud to call her "friend."

My mother Barbara Warren encouraged me every step of the way, praying for me and with me and being the best mom anyone could have. You're my touchstone and I'm blessed.

Kim O'Malley, my best friend for over 35 years, for giving me hints and encouraging the creation of the sweet, or dessert, pretzels—and for occasionally talking me off the ledge. There are angels masquerading as humans, and she's one of them.

Angie Strother (a.k.a. Ang Lee), for the late-night conversations and laughter that kept me typing away and splurfing on my keyboard. Especially for helping me get through the Acai Berry Juice Incident when I thought I had fried my computer. There are worse things that could happen, but I'm glad you have the grace not to tell me about them.

Elaine, Liverwurst, Spooky, Shelley, Roberta: you rock. You know that you do. Thanks for supporting me; couldn't love you any more. If I did, it would be kinda creepy, don't you think? Keep rebuilding your cities, guys. You are awesome and I'm humbled to know you.

My New York posse: David, Bret, Eileen, Vonya, Christie, Nichol, Lovey, Robert, Peter,

Susan, and the gang at Johnny's Bar, for being there with input, whether I wanted it or not and for buying me a drink when I did want one.

My lads at Tea and Sympathy Carry-On, for providing me with candy and laughter during those final dark days when I thought if I had to see one more pretzel I would go mad.

Freddy at my corner store for fronting me when I was completely broke.

The Dice and Walker families, and Mumsy and Papa, for being kind, loving, and appreciating a good laugh.

I'm sure there have been many, many others, so accept my apologies if I've neglected you. I appreciate you and acknowledge you in my heart.

THE LOWDOWN ON PRETZELS

Pretzels are loved by people all over the world. Beer and pretzels, chocolate-covered pretzels, and New York-style soft pretzels with mustard are all favorite snacks for a whole lot of people—except for yours truly. I don't really like pretzels. Never have. But I've always been fascinated with the allure of pretzels. What makes them so appealing to so many people? Just as I was wondering about that, a bit of serendipity occurred. My editor and dear friend Diana von Glahn proposed the idea of this book, and I was reluctant to demur. How can I say no to a project having to do with food when I love to cook? I love to share recipes and I love well-written cookbooks that offer me a different and fun look at common food-stuffs. So why not help create this book, which will help millions of people (hopefully) enjoy the many twists and turns of the world's favorite snack: the pretzel? Since I am creative in the kitchen and like to think of myself as a bit of a gourmet, I thought I was up for the challenge. I wanted to make pretzels appealing to people like me,

the pretzel naysayer. But first, I had to understand this snack.

Research was in order. How did the pretzel become the beloved snack of nations, far and wide? The origins of the pretzel aren't necessarily shrouded in mystery, but, truth be told, there is no definitive story. Here's the lowdown.

The pretzel began, many say, in a monastery in Northern Italy—or was it the French region of Alsace?—sometime around 610 AD. So this doesn't start out well—we're still in the dark as to which country was the birthplace of this beloved snack. Who was it—the Italians or the French? We don't know, so stop asking.

At any rate, the monks of this monastery took scraps of dough and fashioned them into shapes that represented the folded arms of a child in prayer. It is believed that the three spaces represented the Holy Trinity—Father, Son, and Holy Spirit. These baked goods were given to children as a treat (bribe) for learning Scripture and prayers. Called *pretiola*, Latin for "little reward," pretzels soon were called *brachiola* in Italian, which means "little arms." Somehow (again, it's unclear), the *brachiola* made their way to Germany, where they became *bretzel,* or pretzel, as we know them today.

It's said that in medieval times, merchants traveling to the Frankfurt Fair would be greeted by the townspeople with pewter pitchers of wine and tremendous amounts of crisp dough, called *geleit-pretzels,* on the ends of their spears. Since the merchants were always being robbed, the pretzel was yet again being used as a form of bribery, to keep the incoming merchants from disrespecting the townspeople. Now, I can see using food as an inducement, but pretzels? But it makes sense. The pretzel is cost efficient—and after all, there were a lot of palms to grease in those days.

Today, the pretzel is still used as a bribe in bars and taverns worldwide. Think about it—enjoy some salty pretzels and you're likely to want a beverage (or two, or three) to quench your thirst. Smart thinking, barkeep.

In the early days of our nation, German immigrants made the pretzel the popular snack that it is today, bringing them to the cities where they are best known: New York and Philadelphia. You have them to thank for this book, I suppose. The Sturgis Pretzel House in Lititz, Pennsylvania, is the oldest pretzel bakery in the United States, and remains active after more than 140 years in operation. They use the same recipe that they started with and it's just as successful today (be sure to visit it if you have the chance).

The pretzel has come a long way from persuading kids to learn Bible verses, hasn't it?

On my quest to unravel the mystery of the world's favorite snack food, I discovered that there are really only a couple of basic pretzel recipes. The key to making a classic crunchewy (my favorite made-up word) pretzel is with a baking soda or lye bath.

In the old days, German grandmas used to dip pretzel dough in a lye solution. Nowadays, we're not inclined to use lye—to be frank with you, I'm uncomfortable attempting the trial and error until I get the right ratio. Plus, lye is ever so harsh on the hands, and it's far from being kid friendly. (Since this book is meant to be enjoyed by both kids and adults, I've not included lye in any of the recipes in this book.) Baking soda is a great substitute. Here's how it works: When you dip a pretzel into a baking soda bath and put it in the oven, a chemical reaction, known as the *Maillard reaction,* occurs, accelerating the browning and crisping of the exterior of the pretzel. This chemical reaction is very similar to the caramelization process in cooking. It contributes to the overall flavor and consistency of a pretzel. Without this step, your pretzels will be pale and breadlike. So, if you're thinking that you want to forego this step, remember that the end result will not be a pretzel, but a pretzel-shaped bread. Now, you don't want that, do you? So remember that baking soda step. I can't stress that enough.

In this book, I have included a number of delicious and basic recipes for homemade pretzels. I've also done my best to take the humble pretzel and give it a few new culinary twists (sorry, I couldn't resist). I find that these variations on a theme cover the main reasons I like to eat (as quoted by my then 5-year-old nephew, Tristan): *delicion and nutrition*. Food has got to be delicious, and if it's nutritious as well, you're on your way to a fine dining experience. The pretzels recipes you'll find here include pretzels with different toppings, pretzels with great additions mixed right into the dough, sweet and savor stuffed pretzels, pretzel sandwiches—or pretzelwiches, as I call them—and recipes using store-bought pretzels, as well.

Since I like easy recipes, none of the recipes in this book will be too mentally, physically, or emotionally taxing. Once you get past the fear of baking with yeast—if you're one of *those* people—you'll be well on your way to enjoying a number of delicious homemade pretzels whenever you want.

I've been cooking since I was about 5 years old, so there is little that scares me in the kitchen. I know most of what I know due to the patience of my maternal grandmother, who was always so relaxed, and that translated into her cooking. If you feel that baking is a difficult science, never fear. It can be, to be sure, but it's a great deal easier if you can remember that there are no mistakes in the kitchen, only discoveries. Some recipes in this book may call for an ingredient or ingredients you're unfamiliar with, but don't back off—forge ahead! You'll be surprised at the results.

Don't be afraid to experiment. Nothing in this book is written in stone—save for the baking soda bath (is the dead horse beaten enough for you?).

You will discover that it's a good idea to taste anything before you add it—salt and sugar look an awful lot alike. I learned that lesson the hard way. You'll also learn, through experimentation, that some combinations aren't meant to be. For example, a good friend of mine really, really wanted a Guinness-flavored pretzel in this book. It couldn't happen—it ended up tasting like sour socks. Well, I've never eaten a sock, but just imagine a pair of woolen socks drenched in stale beer. Other combinations are a pleasant surprise, like the Turtle Pretzel. Despite my feelings about pretzels, this one brought me immense pleasure, I can tell you.

I've also included some fun facts about pretzels throughout the book—although some might be a little exaggerated. So while you're baking, you're learning.

There are also many kid friendly recipes in this book that will make cooking a fun adventure for you and your whole family (or your neighbor's family). Nothing is more fun than watching a child accomplish something in the kitchen. It's a wonderful way to bond and create cherished memories.

In the end, you should have fun with this book. Refer to it when you're looking for something yummy to spice up your weekly menu, as well as when you're craving pretzels. There's no excuse for not getting in that kitchen and whipping up a pretzel creation.

And now, after my many-month-long exploration of pretzelry, you might want to know what I've learned? Pretzels are pretty good things. I don't fear the pretzel any longer. I have made friends with the pretzel. There's more to pretzels than I thought and I'm glad that I can share these recipes with you. Enjoy!

A Quick Note About Substitutions

The flour used for these recipes is always all-purpose flour unless otherwise indicated. You can use unbleached flour, but don't use cake flour or self-rising flour. Cake flour will not provide the desired results because it has a lighter texture. Self-rising flour has baking powder in it and that will impact the measurements in the pretzel dough. Unless you are a seasoned baker, don't try it for pretzels.

CONFECTIONERS' (POWDERED) SUGAR: If you don't have any on hand, use this trick— for every cup of confectioners' sugar required, combine 1 cup sugar with 1 tablespoon cornstarch in the blender and blast it until you have a powdery product.

FRESH VERSUS DRIED HERBS: The use of fresh herbs is generally something I advocate, but if you can't find the particular herb listed in any of the recipes, use a smaller amount of the dried herb. Remember that dried herbs are intense in flavor—so less is more. For every tablespoon of fresh herbs, use 1 teaspoon of dried or ¾ teaspoon ground herbs.

PANCETTA: This cured pork belly is like bacon, and can often be found at the deli counter of your local grocery. If you can't find it or if it's just too expensive in your area, use slab bacon.

PRETZEL SHAPING 101

Before you begin shaping your dough, decide if you're making large pretzels, small pretzels, or pretzel bites.

TO MAKE LARGE PRETZELS, which bake out to about 6 to 7 inches wide, use a sharp knife or dough scraper to cut the dough into 6 pieces. Use your hands to roll each piece into a rope that is about 24 inches long and 2 inches thick.

TO MAKE SMALL PRETZELS, which bake out to about 4 to 5 inches wide, cut the dough into about 12 pieces. Depending on the size you cut them, you may be able to make up to 16 pretzels. Use your hands to roll each piece into a rope that is about 12 inches long and 2 inches thick.

TO MAKE PRETZEL BITES, which bake to about 2 inches square, cut the dough into 6 pieces, then use your hands to roll each piece into a 12-inch rope about 1 inch thick. Cut each rope into 1-inch pieces. This should make about 36 to 48 pretzel bites.

Shaping pretzels can be a fun way to unleash your creativity while making delicious and nutritious snacks for you and your friends and family to enjoy. Here are some instructions and ideas for shaping your pretzel dough.

THE CLASSIC (NEW YORK) PRETZEL: Take each dough rope and form it into a U-shape, with the bend facing away from you and the ends pointing at you. Take the ends and cross them. Grab the top of the bend and carefully bring it up and over the ends, essentially folding the pretzel in half, toward you. Gently press the dough where it meets to secure it together.

THE PHILLY SPECIAL: Take each dough rope and place it vertically on your workspace, so one of the ends is facing you and one is pointing away from you. Fold each end in, so they meet in the middle of the rope, essentially forming a figure 8, without the holes. Secure the ends into the center of the dough by pressing gently.

CLASSIC, WITH A TWIST: Take each dough rope and form it into a U-shape, with the bend facing away from you and the ends pointing at you. Take one of the ends and bend it diagonally so it lays across the top left side of the U bend. Take the other end and bend it so it crosses the first piece and sits on the top right corner of the bend. Gently press the dough where it meets to secure it together.

THE PRETZEL BRAID: Take three dough ropes and place them vertically on your workspace, so three of the ends are facing you and three are pointing away from you. Gently braid the ropes: take the rope on the left and cross it over the middle rope. Take the rope on the right and cross it over the middle rope. Continue in this manner until the ropes are completely braided. Secure the ends together by gently pressing on them.

THE PRETZEL TWIST: Take two dough ropes and place them vertically on your workspace, so two of the ends are facing you and two are pointing away from you. Gently twist the ropes, taking the rope on the left and crossing it over the rope on the right. Continue in this manner until the ropes are completely twisted. Secure the ends together by gently pressing on them.

PRETZEL NUMBERS AND LETTERS: Take each dough rope and cut it in half. Shape letters and numbers as you desire.

- **BE SURE TO** punch out the air from the dough before you begin shaping your pretzels. As your dough rises, air pockets form inside your dough, which makes for light dough on the inside. But it can also make it difficult to roll the dough into logs. After letting the dough rise over night, punch it down and begin shaping. When you shape your pretzels, you'll let them rise again, so you don't have to worry about making pretzels that are too dense.

- **DOUGH EXPANDS AS** it bakes, so take that into account as you shape your dough. For instance, if you're trying to form the classic pretzel shape, with holes in between the dough "arms", you have to make sure to shape your pretzel with bigger holes that you'd expect after the pretzel is baked.

- **ONCE YOUR DOUGH** has risen, the gluten in your dough will tense up, and may make it difficult for you to roll out the logs to their necessary length. If this happens, let the log sit and you continue with the others, then return to it. This will allow the gluten to rest, and enable you to continue to stretch it to the necessary length.

PRETZEL PARTIES

When my kids were younger, my friend Teresa would have cookie parties at Christmastime. All of the kids would get half a dozen cookies and all sorts of different toppings and icings to decorate their plain sugar cookies. It was loads of fun for the kids. Pretzel parties are a take on that concept.

Obviously, the easiest way to prep for the party is to buy frozen bread dough and thaw it overnight. Of course, if you're enterprising, or don't expect a lot of kids at your party, you can make a few batches of dough (and dipping sauces, if you like) from this book to suit your guests. Be sure to make a couple batches of the chocolate dough for those who enjoy sweets.

Help your guests shape their pretzels into any number of fun shapes, following the directions on pages 18-19, or help them create their own ideas.

Topping ideas are limitless—the best bet is to use whatever takes your fancy. But if you need some help, check out the list of suggestions on page 24.

Have plenty of paper towels on hand—this is sure to get messy, but it is absolutely worth it to see the delight on your guests' faces.

PRETZELS, PLAIN AND SIMPLE

Basic Pretzels

1 tablespoon active dry yeast

1 cup warm water (100 to 115°F), plus more if needed

4 tablespoons light brown sugar

3½ cups all-purpose flour

2 teaspoons salt

2 teaspoons baking soda

1 cup hot water

1 egg, lightly beaten

Toppings (see suggestions below)

In a large mixing bowl, combine the yeast, water, and 1 tablespoon brown sugar (see Proofing Yeast below).

Add the remaining brown sugar and mix until well incorporated. Add the flour and salt and mix with your hands or a wooden spoon until the mixture forms a smooth dough. If the mixture is dry, add 1 or 2 tablespoons water. Knead the dough until smooth, about 7 to 8 minutes. Place the dough in a bowl sprayed with nonstick cooking spray, cover with plastic wrap, and let it rest overnight in the refrigerator.

Punch the dough down, then turn it out onto a lightly floured work surface and cut
it into pieces, depending on the size and type of pretzel you want to make. Follow the directions on pages 18-19 to shape the pretzels. Place the pretzels on a parchment-lined baking sheet, cover them with plastic wrap, and let them rise at room temperature for 45 minutes, or until they have doubled in size.

Preheat the oven to 450°F.

Combine the baking soda and hot water in a bowl. Dip the risen pretzels in the baking soda bath, then return them to the baking sheet and brush them with egg. Sprinkle with the desired toppings.

Bake the pretzels for 15 minutes, or until they are golden brown. Let them cool on the baking sheet for 5 to 10 minutes before eating.

PROOFING YEAST: To proof yeast—or to make sure it is still active—add the yeast to the warm water called for in the recipe. Remember that "warm" is between 110 and 115°F. If the water is too hot, it will kill the yeast; if it is not warm enough, it won't awaken the yeast. Add 1 tablespoon of the sugar called for in the recipe and let the mixture sit for 5 minutes. When the yeast is foamy and smells like bread, it's active and you can move on with the recipe.

Topping Creativity

CLASSIC PRETZELS: Sprinkle the pretzels with ¼ cup kosher salt , then bake as directed in the recipe.

SESAME SEED PRETZELS: Sprinkle the pretzels with ¼ cup sesame seeds. Bake at 400°F for 15 minutes, or until they are golden brown and crunchy.

POPPY SEED PRETZELS: Sprinkle the pretzels with ¼ cup poppy seeds. Bake at 400°F for 15 minutes, or until they are golden brown and crunchy.

CARAWAY SEED PRETZELS: Sprinkle the pretzels with ¼ cup caraway seeds. Bake at 400°F for 15 minutes, or until they are golden brown and crunchy.

GARLIC PRETZELS: Sprinkle the pretzels with 4 minced cloves of garlic. Bake at 450°F for 15 minutes, or until they are golden brown and crunchy.

SUNFLOWER SEED PRETZELS: After you brush the pretzels with egg wash, brush them with 3 tablespoons melted butter. Sprinkle them with 3 tablespoons kosher salt and ¼ cup shelled sunflower seeds. Bake at 450°F for 15 minutes, or until they are golden brown and crunchy.

CAJUN-SPICED PRETZELS: Combine ¼ cup salt, 1 teaspoon cayenne pepper, ½ teaspoon paprika, 1 teaspoon onion powder, 1 teaspoon garlic powder, ½ teaspoon white pepper, 1 teaspoon chili powder, ⅛ teaspoon dried thyme, and a pinch of sugar. Sprinkle over the pretzels and bake at 450°F for 15 minutes, or until they are golden brown and crunchy.

ANISEED PRETZELS: Sprinkle the pretzels with ½ cup aniseseed. Bake at 450°F for 15 minutes, or until they are golden brown and crunchy. Alternatively, add aniseseed to the dough, and sprinkle with an additional amount of aniseseed before baking.

FLAXSEED PRETZELS: Sprinkle the pretzels with 1 cup of flaxseed. Bake at 450°F for 15 minutes, or until they are golden brown and crunchy.

THE EVERYTHING PRETZEL: Combine 2 tablespoons sesame seeds, 2 tablespoons poppy seeds, 2 tablespoons caraway seeds, ¼ cup minced onion, 2 minced garlic cloves, 2 tablespoons sunflower seeds, and 2 tablespoons kosher salt. Sprinkle over the pretzels and bake at 450°F for 15 minutes, or until they are golden brown and crunchy.

Garlic Butter Pretzels

1 batch Basic Pretzel dough (page 23)

2 teaspoons baking soda

1 cup hot water

1 egg, lightly beaten

¼ pound (1 stick) butter, melted

3 garlic cloves, minced

Prepare the pretzel dough as directed in the recipe.

Place the dough in a bowl sprayed with nonstick cooking spray, cover with plastic wrap, and let it rest overnight in the refrigerator.

Punch the dough down, then turn it out onto a lightly floured work surface and cut it into pieces, depending on the size and type of pretzel you want to make. Follow the directions on pages 18-19 to shape the pretzels. Place the pretzels on a parchment-lined baking sheet, cover them with plastic wrap, and let them rise at room temperature for 45 minutes, or until they have doubled in size.

Preheat the oven to 400°F.

Combine the baking soda and hot water in a bowl. Dip the risen pretzels in the baking soda bath then dip them in the butter. Return them to the baking sheet and sprinkle them with garlic.

Bake the pretzels for 15 minutes, or until they are golden brown. Let them cool on the baking sheet for 5 to 10 minutes, then dip them in butter and enjoy.

Onion Pretzels

1 batch Basic Pretzel dough
(page 23)

3 tablespoons extra-virgin
olive oil

1 cup minced yellow onion

2 garlic cloves, minced

2 teaspoons baking soda

1 cup hot water

1 egg, lightly beaten

Prepare the pretzel dough as directed in the recipe.

Place the dough in a bowl sprayed with nonstick cooking spray, cover with plastic wrap, and let it rest overnight in the refrigerator.

Punch the dough down, then turn it out onto a lightly floured work surface and cut it into pieces, depending on the size and type of pretzel you want to make. Follow the directions on pages 18–19 to shape the pretzels. Place the pretzels on a parchment-lined baking sheet, cover them with plastic wrap, and let them rise at room temperature for 45 minutes, or until they have doubled in size.

Preheat the oven to 400°F.

In a medium-sized skillet, heat the olive oil over medium heat, then add the onion and garlic. Sauté until the onions are translucent, about 7 minutes. (To caramelize the onions, cook them for about 12 minutes, until the liquid is gone and the onions are deep brown, or caramel colored.) Set aside to cool.

Combine the baking soda and hot water in a bowl. Dip the risen pretzels in the baking soda bath, then return them to the baking sheet and brush them with egg. Spread the cooled onion mixture over them.

Bake the pretzels for 15 minutes, or until they are golden brown. Let them cool on the baking sheet for 5 to 10 minutes before eating.

Jalapeño Pepper and Jack Cheese Pretzels

1 tablespoon active dry yeast

1 cup warm water (100 to 115°F), plus more if needed

4 tablespoons light brown sugar

3½ cups all-purpose flour

2 teaspoons salt

1½ cups shredded Monterey Jack cheese

1½ cups minced jalapeño pepper, or to taste

2 teaspoons baking soda

1 cup hot water

1 egg, lightly beaten

In a large mixing bowl, combine the yeast, water, and 1 tablespoon brown sugar (see Proofing Yeast on page 23).

Add the remaining brown sugar and mix until well incorporated.

Add the flour, salt, 1 cup of the cheese, and 1 cup of the jalapeño and mix until the mixture forms a smooth dough. Place the dough in a bowl sprayed with nonstick cooking spray, cover with plastic wrap, and let it rest overnight in the refrigerator.

Punch the dough down, then turn it out onto a lightly floured work surface and cut it into pieces, depending on the size and type of pretzel you want to make. Follow the directions on pages 18–19 to shape the pretzels. Place the pretzels on a parchment-lined baking sheet, cover them with plastic wrap, and let them rise at room temperature for 45 minutes, or until they have doubled in size.

Preheat the oven to 450°F.

Combine the baking soda and hot water in a bowl. Dip the risen pretzels in the baking soda bath, then return them to the baking sheet and brush them with egg. Sprinkle with the remaining ½ cup of cheese and jalapeño.

Bake the pretzels for 15 minutes, or until they are golden brown. Let them cool on the baking sheet for 5 to 10 minutes before eating.

Pizza Pretzels

1 tablespoon active dry yeast

1 cup warm water (100 to 115°F), plus more if needed

4 tablespoons light brown sugar

3½ cups all-purpose flour

2 teaspoons salt

2 teaspoons dried rosemary

1 teaspoon dried oregano

1 teaspoon dried basil

1 teaspoon dried parsley

1 cup sun-dried tomatoes packed in oil, drained and minced

2 teaspoons baking soda

1 cup hot water

1 (14-ounce) jar pizza sauce

2 cups shredded mozzarella cheese

1½ cups cooked meat of your choice, such as pepperoni or sausage, diced

1 egg, lightly beaten

In a large mixing bowl, combine the yeast, water, and 1 tablespoon brown sugar (see Proofing Yeast on page 23).

Add the remaining brown sugar and mix until well incorporated.

Add the flour, salt, rosemary, oregano, basil, parsley, and tomatoes, and mix until the mixture forms a smooth dough. Place the dough in a bowl sprayed with nonstick cooking spray, cover with plastic wrap, and let it rest overnight in the refrigerator.

Punch the dough down, then turn it out onto a lightly floured work surface. Follow the directions on pages 18–19 to shape the pretzels. Place the pretzels on a parchment-lined baking sheet, cover them with plastic wrap, and let them rise at room temperature for 45 minutes, or until they have doubled in size.

Preheat the oven to 400°F.

Combine the baking soda and hot water in a bowl. Dip the risen pretzels in the baking soda bath. Using a rolling pin or grease hands, flatten the pretzels slightly. Carefully spread pizza sauce over the flattened tops of the pretzels, then sprinkle with the cheese and meat. Brush any exposed pretzel dough with egg.

Bake the pretzels for 20 minutes, or until the crust is golden brown and the cheese is bubbly. Let them cool for 5 to 10 minutes before eating.

Buffalo Pretzels

1 batch Basic Pretzel dough
(page 23)

2 teaspoons baking soda

1 cup hot water

3 ounces hot sauce

¼ pound (1 stick) butter, melted

Blue Cheese Pretzel Dip
(page 165), for serving

Celery stalks, for serving

Prepare the pretzel dough as directed in the recipe.

Place the dough in a bowl sprayed with nonstick cooking spray, cover with plastic wrap, and let it rest overnight in the refrigerator.

Punch the dough down, then turn it out onto a lightly floured work surface and cut it into pieces, depending on the size and type of pretzel you want to make. Follow the directions on pages 18–19 to shape the pretzels. Place the pretzels on a parchment-lined baking sheet, cover them with plastic wrap, and let them rise at room temperature for 45 minutes, or until they have doubled in size.

Preheat the oven to 400°F.

Combine the baking soda and hot water in a bowl. Combine the hot sauce and butter in a separate bowl. Dip the risen pretzels in the baking soda bath then dip them in the hot sauce.

Bake the pretzels for 15 minutes, or until they are golden brown.

Dip the warm pretzels in butter again, and let cool before serving with Blue Cheese Sauce and celery stalks.

THAT'S A LOT OF PRETZELS! According to Wikipedia, more than 300 million pounds of pretzels and pretzel products are produced every year. Annual pretzel sales top $180 million, making the pretzel the second most popular snack in the United States, just behind the potato chip. Each person supposedly eats roughly 1.5 pounds of pretzels each year. In Pennsylvania, people supposedly eat 12 times that amount!

Whole Wheat Pretzels

2½ cups milk

½ cup sugar

¼ cup canola or vegetable oil

1½ teaspoons salt

3 cups all-purpose flour

1 (¼-ounce) package active dry yeast

3 cups whole wheat flour

2 teaspoons baking soda

1 cup hot water

1 egg white, lightly beaten

Toppings (page 24)

In a medium-sized saucepan, heat the milk, sugar, oil, and salt until just warm (about 100 to 115°F).

In a large mixing bowl, combine 2 cups of all-purpose flour and the yeast. Add the warm milk mixture and beat with an electric mixer on low speed for about 1 minute, scraping the bowl. Beat on high for 3 minutes.

Add the whole wheat flour and the remaining all-purpose flour ½ cup at a time, mixing by hand, until it forms a moderately stiff dough.

Punch the dough down, then turn it out onto a floured surface and knead until smooth, about 5 minutes. Shape the dough into a ball and place in a greased bowl, turning once so the entire surface of the dough is greased. Cover with plastic wrap or a clean kitchen towel and let the dough rise at room temperature for 1 hour, or until it doubles in size.

Punch the dough down and turn it out onto a floured surface. Cover with plastic wrap or a clean kitchen towel and let it rest for 10 minutes.

Preheat the oven to 350°F.

Cut the dough into pieces, depending on the size and type of pretzel you want to make. Follow the directions on pages 18-19 to shape the pretzels.

Combine the baking soda and hot water in a bowl. Dip the risen pretzels in the baking soda bath, then return them to the baking sheet and brush them with egg white. Sprinkle with the desired toppings.

Bake the pretzels for 20 minutes, or until they are golden brown. Let them cool on the baking sheet for 5 to 10 minutes before eating.

Soy Flour Pretzels

1 (¼-ounce) package active
  dry yeast

1½ cups warm water
  (100 to 115°F)

1¼ tablespoons sugar

1¼ teaspoons salt

4 cups all-purpose flour

2 tablespoons soy flour

1 egg, lightly beaten

Toppings (page 24)

In a large bowl, combine the yeast, water, and sugar (see Proofing Yeast on page 23). Stir until well incorporated.

Add the salt and both flours and mix well with an electric mixer on low speed or by hand.

Preheat the oven to 425°F.

Punch the dough down, then turn it out onto a lightly floured work surface and knead until the dough is smooth and elastic, about 7 minutes. Cut the dough into pieces, depending on the size and type of pretzel you want to make. Follow the directions on pages 18–19 to shape the pretzels. Place the pretzels on a parchment-lined baking sheet, brush them with egg, and sprinkle with the desired topping.

Bake the pretzels for 15 minutes, or until they are light brown in color. Let them cool on the baking sheet for 5 to 10 minutes before eating.

DID YOU KNOW?
The number one topping for a soft pretzel is mustard. Some people enjoy pretzels with ketchup, but they are scoffed at by pretzel purists.

Bran Pretzels

1½ cups warm water
  (100 to 115°F)

1 cup 100% bran

1 tablespoon butter, softened

3½ cups all-purpose flour,
  plus more as needed

1 (¼-ounce) package active
  dry yeast

1 tablespoon sugar

1 teaspoon salt

2 teaspoons baking soda

1 cup hot water

1 egg, lightly beaten

Toppings (page 24)

In a small bowl, combine the water, bran, and butter. Set aside.

In a large bowl, combine 1½ cups of the flour, the yeast, sugar, and salt. Stir the bran mixture into the dry ingredients. Add the remaining 2 cups flour, ½ cup at a time, and combine to make a soft dough.

Punch the dough down, then turn it out onto a floured surface and knead lightly for 5 minutes, or until it is smooth and elastic. If the dough is too sticky, add more flour, 1 teaspoon at a time. Cover the dough with plastic wrap or a clean kitchen towel and let it rest for 10 minutes.

Cut the dough into pieces, depending on the size and type of pretzel you want to make. Follow the directions on pages 18-19 to shape the pretzels. Place the pretzels on a parchment-lined baking sheet, cover them with plastic wrap, and let them rise for 30 minutes, or until they have doubled in size.

Preheat the oven to 450°F.

Combine the baking soda and hot water in a bowl. Dip the risen pretzels in the baking soda bath, then return them to the baking sheet and brush them with egg. Sprinkle with the desired toppings.

Bake the pretzels for 15 minutes, or until they are golden brown. Let them cool on the baking sheet for 5 to 10 minutes before eating.

Sari's Gluten-Free Pretzels

2 (¼-ounce) packages active
dry yeast

2 cups warm water
(100 to 115°F)

1 teaspoon brown sugar

½ teaspoon sea salt

2 cups brown rice flour

1 cup tapioca flour

1 cup plus 1 teaspoon
potato starch

4 teaspoons xanthan gum

2 teaspoons baking soda

½ cup warm water
(100 to 115°F)

Toppings (page 24)

Melted butter, for serving

Mix the yeast, 1½ cups of the warm water, brown sugar, and sea salt in a large bowl and set aside for 5 minutes (see Proofing Yeast on page 23).

In a medium-sized bowl, combine the rice flour, tapioca flour, potato starch, and xanthan gum. Pour half of the dry mixture into the yeast mixture and mix on low speed with an electric mixer for 3 minutes, or until the ingredients are well blended. Add the remaining dry mixture and mix until well incorporated.

Place the dough in a bowl sprayed with nonstick cooking spray, cover with plastic wrap, and let the dough rise at room temperature for 1 hour.

Preheat the oven to 500°F.

Combine the baking soda and remaining ½ cup warm water in a medium-sized bowl.

Punch the dough down, then turn it out onto a lightly floured work surface and cut it into 8, 16, or 48 pieces, depending on the size and type of pretzel you want to make. Follow the directions on pages 18-19 to shape the pretzels. This dough is much more delicate than dough prepared with all-purpose flour. It will crumble more easily, so be careful to let the dough rest on the work surface as you shape the pretzels. If parts of the dough feel dry, add a couple of drops of the baking soda water to your palm as you work.

Carefully dip the pretzels in the baking soda bath and place on a parchment-lined baking sheet. Sprinkle with the desired toppings.

Bake the pretzels for 8 minutes, or until they are lightly brown. These pretzels do not brown as darkly as other pretzels.

Serve immediately with melted butter for dipping.

The Cheater: Bread Dough Pretzel

1 (16-ounce) loaf frozen bread
    dough, thawed

2 teaspoons baking soda

1 cup hot water

1 egg, lightly beaten

Toppings (page 24)

4 to 5 cups boiling water

Preheat the oven to 350°F.

Cut the bread dough into pieces, depending on the size and type of pretzel you want to make. Follow the directions on pages 18-19 to shape the pretzels. Place them on a parchment-lined baking sheet, cover them with plastic wrap, and let them rise for 20 minutes.

Combine the baking soda and hot water in a bowl. Dip the risen pretzels in the baking soda bath, then return them to the baking sheet and brush them with egg. Sprinkle with the desired toppings.

Place a shallow pan containing 1-inch of boiling water on the bottom rack of the oven. Bake the pretzels over the pan of water for 20 minutes or until they are golden brown. Let them cool on the baking sheet for 5 to 10 minutes before eating.

MIX-INS: PRETZELS OF A DIFFERENT FLAVOR

Parmesan Cheese Pretzels

1 batch Basic Pretzel dough
(page 23)

1½ cups mixed shredded and
grated Parmesan cheese

2 teaspoons baking soda

1 cup hot water

1 egg, lightly beaten

Prepare the pretzel dough as directed in the recipe, adding 1 cup of the cheese as you mix the proofed yeast with the flour.

Place the dough in a bowl sprayed with nonstick cooking spray, cover with plastic wrap, and let it rest overnight in the refrigerator.

Punch the dough down, then turn it out onto a lightly floured work surface and cut it into pieces, depending on the size and type of pretzel you want to make. Follow the directions on pages 18–19 to shape the pretzels. Place the pretzels on a parchment–lined baking sheet, cover them with plastic wrap, and let them rise at room temperature for 45 minutes, or until they have doubled in size.

Preheat the oven to 450°F.

Combine the baking soda and hot water in a bowl. Dip the risen pretzels in the baking soda bath, then return them to the baking sheet and brush them with egg. Sprinkle with the remaining ½ cup cheese.

Bake the pretzels for 15 minutes, or until they are golden brown. Let them cool on the baking sheet for 5 to 10 minutes before eating.

Italian Herb Pretzels

1 batch Basic Pretzel dough
  (page 23)

2 teaspoons dried rosemary

1 teaspoon dried oregano

1 teaspoon dried basil

1 teaspoon dried parsley

2 teaspoons baking soda

1 cup hot water

Toppings (page 24)

Prepare the pretzel dough as directed in the recipe, adding the herbs as you mix the proofed yeast with the flour.

Place the dough in a bowl sprayed with nonstick cooking spray, cover with plastic wrap, and let it rest overnight in the refrigerator.

Punch the dough down, then turn it out onto a lightly floured work surface and cut it into pieces, depending on the size and type of pretzel you want to make. Follow the directions on pages 18–19 to shape the pretzels. Place the pretzels on a parchment-lined baking sheet, cover them with plastic wrap, and let them rise at room temperature for 45 minutes, or until they have doubled in size.

Preheat the oven to 450°F.

Combine the baking soda and hot water in a bowl. Dip the risen pretzels in the baking soda bath, then return them to the baking sheet and brush them brush them with egg. Sprinkle with the desired toppings.

Bake the pretzels for 15 minutes, or until they are golden brown. Let them cool on the baking sheet for 5 to 10 minutes before eating.

VARIATIONS ON THIS THEME:

HERB AND GARLIC PRETZELS: Mince 2 garlic cloves and add it to the dough along with the herbs. Be sure to mix thoroughly to distribute the garlic.

SUN-DRIED TOMATO AND HERB PRETZELS: Add 1 cup of drained and minced sun-dried tomatoes to the dough along with the herbs. Bake the pretzels at 400°F for 15 minutes, or until they are golden brown. Let them cool on the baking sheet for 5 to 10 minutes before eating.

Ranch Pretzels

1 batch Basic Pretzel dough
(page 23)

1 (0.4-ounce) package
powdered ranch dressing mix

2 teaspoons baking soda

1 cup hot water

4 tablespoons butter, melted

Prepare the pretzel dough as directed in the recipe, adding half the ranch dressing as you mix the proofed yeast with the flour.

Place the dough in a bowl sprayed with nonstick cooking spray, cover with plastic wrap, and let it rest overnight in the refrigerator.

Punch the dough down, then turn it out onto a lightly floured work surface and cut it into pieces, depending on the size and type of pretzel you want to make. Follow the directions on pages 18-19 to shape the pretzels. Place the pretzels on a parchment-lined baking sheet, cover them with plastic wrap, and let them rise at room temperature for 45 minutes, or until they have doubled in size.

Preheat the oven to 450°F.

Combine the baking soda and hot water in a bowl. Dip the pretzels in the baking soda bath, then return them to the baking sheet and brush them with butter. Sprinkle with the remaining ranch dressing.

Bake the pretzels for 15 minutes, or until they are golden brown. Let them cool on the baking sheet for 5 to 10 minutes before eating.

HAPPY PRETZEL NEW YEAR!

On New Year's Day, the children of early Pennsylvania Dutch settlers would tie pretzels on a string and wear them around their necks for good luck.

Chocolate Pretzels

PRETZELS

1 tablespoon active dry yeast

1 cup warm water (100 to 115°F), plus more if needed

¼ cup light brown sugar

3¼ cups all-purpose flour

¼ cup Dutch-processed cocoa

2 teaspoons salt

2 tablespoons sugar

1 teaspoon vanilla extract

1½ cups chocolate chips, milk or semisweet

2 teaspoons baking soda

1 cup hot water

1 egg, lightly beaten

FROSTING

1 cup confectioners' sugar

1 teaspoon vanilla extract

3 tablespoons sour cream

4 tablespoons butter, softened

In a large mixing bowl, combine the yeast, water, and 1 tablespoon brown sugar (see Proofing Yeast on page 23).

Add the remaining brown sugar and mix until well incorporated.

Add the flour, cocoa, salt, sugar, and vanilla, and mix until the mixture forms a smooth dough. Add the chocolate chips and mix to combine. Place the dough in a bowl sprayed with nonstick cooking spray, cover with plastic wrap, and let it rest overnight in the refrigerator.

Punch the dough down, then turn it out onto a lightly floured work surface and cut it into pieces, depending on the size and type of pretzel you want to make. Follow the directions on pages 18–19 to shape the pretzels. Place the pretzels on a parchment-lined baking sheet, cover them with plastic wrap, and let them rise at room temperature for 45 minutes, or until they have doubled in size.

Preheat the oven to 450°F.

Combine the baking soda and hot water in a bowl. Dip the risen pretzels in the baking soda bath, then return them to the baking sheet and brush them with egg.

Bake the pretzels for 15 minutes, checking for doneness after the 12 minute mark. Since these pretzels are naturally dark in color, they scorch easily. Let the pretzels cool while you prepare the frosting.

Combine the confectioners' sugar, vanilla, sour cream, and butter in a large bowl and mix until smooth. Drizzle over the pretzels.

Cinnamon Pretzels

- -

1 tablespoon active dry yeast

1 cup warm water (100 to 115°F), plus more if needed

¼ cup light brown sugar

3½ cups all-purpose flour

2 teaspoons salt

5 tablespoons ground cinnamon

½ cup sugar

2 teaspoons baking soda

1 cup hot water

1 egg, lightly beaten

In a large mixing bowl, combine the yeast, water, and 1 tablespoon brown sugar (see Proofing Yeast on page 23).

Add the remaining brown sugar and mix until well incorporated.

Add the flour, salt, and 2 tablespoons of the cinnamon and mix until the mixture forms a smooth dough. Place the dough in a bowl sprayed with nonstick cooking spray, cover with plastic wrap, and let it rest overnight in the refrigerator.

Punch the dough down, then turn it out onto a lightly floured work surface and cut it into pieces, depending on the size and type of pretzel you want to make. Follow the directions on pages 18-19 to shape the pretzels. Place the pretzels on a parchment-lined baking sheet, cover them with plastic wrap, and let them rise at room temperature for 45 minutes, or until they have doubled in size.

Preheat the oven to 450°F.

Combine the sugar with the remaining 3 tablespoons of cinnamon.

Combine the baking soda and hot water in a bowl. Dip the risen pretzels in the baking soda bath, then return them to the baking sheet and brush them with egg. Sprinkle with cinnamon sugar.

Bake the pretzels for 15 minutes, or until they are golden brown. Let them cool on the baking sheet for 5 to 10 minutes before eating.

Butterscotch Pretzels

1 tablespoon active dry yeast

1 cup warm water (100 to 115°F), plus more if needed

¼ cup light brown sugar

3¼ cups all-purpose flour

¼ cup Dutch-processed cocoa

2 teaspoons salt

2 tablespoons sugar

1 teaspoon vanilla extract

1 cup butterscotch chips

2 teaspoons baking soda

1 cup hot water

1 egg, lightly beaten

In a large mixing bowl, combine the yeast, water, and 1 tablespoon brown sugar (see Proofing Yeast on page 23).

Add the remaining brown sugar and mix until well incorporated.

Add the flour, cocoa, salt, sugar, and vanilla, and mix until the mixture forms a smooth dough. Add the butterscotch chips and stir to combine. Place the dough in a bowl sprayed with nonstick cooking spray, cover with plastic wrap, and let it rest overnight in the refrigerator.

Punch the dough down, then turn it out onto a lightly floured work surface and cut it into pieces, depending on the size and type of pretzel you want to make. Follow the directions on pages 18–19 to shape the pretzels. Place the pretzels on a parchment-lined baking sheet, cover them with plastic wrap, and let them rise at room temperature for 45 minutes, or until they have doubled in size.

Preheat the oven to 450°F.

Combine the baking soda and hot water in a bowl. Dip the risen pretzels in the baking soda bath, then return them to the baking sheet and brush them with egg.

Bake the pretzels for 15 minutes, checking for doneness after the 12 minute mark. Since these pretzels are naturally dark in color, they scorch easily. Let them cool on the baking sheet for 5 to 10 minutes before eating.

Five-Flavor Pretzels

1 batch Basic Pretzel dough
(page 23)

1 tablespoon almond extract

1 tablespoon butter extract

1 tablespoon rum extract

1 tablespoon vanilla extract

1 tablespoon coconut extract

2 teaspoons baking soda

1 cup hot water

1 egg, lightly beaten

Toppings (page 24)

Prepare the pretzel dough as directed in the recipe, adding all of the extracts as you mix the proofed yeast with the flour.

Place the dough in a bowl sprayed with nonstick cooking spray, cover with plastic wrap, and let it rest overnight in the refrigerator.

Punch the dough down, then turn it out onto a lightly floured work surface and cut it into pieces, depending on the size and type of pretzel you want to make. Follow the directions on pages 18-19 to shape the pretzels. Place the pretzels on a parchment-lined baking sheet, cover them with plastic wrap, and let them rise at room temperature for 45 minutes, or until they have doubled in size.

Preheat the oven to 450°F.

Combine the baking soda and hot water in a bowl. Dip the risen pretzels in the baking soda bath, then return them to the baking sheet and brush them with egg. Sprinkle with the desired toppings.

Bake the pretzels for 15 minutes, or until they are golden brown. Let them cool on the baking sheet for 5 to 10 minutes before eating.

Almond Pretzels

1 batch Basic Pretzel dough
(page 23)

2 teaspoons almond extract

2 teaspoons baking soda

1 cup hot water

1 egg, lightly beaten

1 cup sliced almonds

Prepare the pretzel dough as directed in the recipe, adding the almond extract as you mix the proofed yeast with the flour.

Place the dough in a bowl sprayed with nonstick cooking spray, cover with plastic wrap, and let it rest overnight in the refrigerator.

Punch the dough down, then turn it out onto a lightly floured work surface and cut it into pieces, depending on the size and type of pretzel you want to make. Follow the directions on pages 18-19 to shape the pretzels. Place the pretzels on a parchment-lined baking sheet, cover them with plastic wrap, and let them rise at room temperature for 45 minutes, or until they have doubled in size.

Preheat the oven to 450°F.

Combine the baking soda and hot water in a bowl. Dip the risen pretzels in the baking soda bath, then return them to the baking sheet and brush them with egg. Sprinkle with the sliced almonds.

Bake the pretzels for 15 minutes, or until they are golden brown. Let them cool on the baking sheet for 5 to 10 minutes before eating.

PRETZEL BAKERS SAVE THE DAY!

Did you know that pretzel bakers have a coat of arms?
A shield emblazoned with a charging lion and a pretzel was awarded to some pretzel bakers in Vienna during the sixteenth century. Turks who had been unsuccessful in their attempts to storm a Viennese city's walls decided to tunnel in. Pretzel bakers, working diligently in the middle of the night, heard the noise and alerted the guards. The city was saved and the emperor rewarded the cunning bakers with the crest that is still used today.

Almond Joy Pretzel Bites

1 tablespoon active dry yeast

1 cup warm water (100 to 115°F), plus more if needed

¼ cup light brown sugar

3¼ cups all-purpose flour

¼ cup Dutch-processed cocoa

2 teaspoons salt

2 tablespoons sugar

2 teaspoons vanilla extract

1 teaspoon almond extract

2 cups semisweet chocolate chips

½ cup sweetened coconut flakes

8 ounces almond paste

½ cup blanched almonds, finely chopped

¼ cup confectioners' sugar

1 large egg white

2 teaspoons baking soda

1 cup hot water

1 egg, lightly beaten

Frosting (page 40), optional

In a large mixing bowl, combine the yeast, water, and brown sugar (see Proofing Yeast on page 23). Stir until well incorporated.

Add the flour, cocoa, salt, and sugar, and mix with an electric mixer on medium speed for 5 minutes, or until the mixture forms a smooth dough. Add the vanilla and almond extracts, the chocolate chips, coconut flakes, almond paste, blanched almonds, confectioners' sugar, and egg white, and stir by hand to combine.

Place the dough in a bowl sprayed with nonstick cooking spray, cover with plastic wrap, and let it rest overnight in the refrigerator.

Punch the dough down, then turn it out onto a lightly floured work surface and cut it into 6 pieces. Use your hands to roll the dough into ropes that are about 24 inches long and 2 inches thick. Cut each rope into 1-inch pieces. Place the dough pieces on a parchment-lined baking sheet, cover them with plastic wrap, and let them rise at room temperature for 45 minutes, or until they have doubled in size.

Preheat the oven to 450°F.

Combine the baking soda and hot water in a bowl. Dip the risen pretzels in the baking soda bath, then return them to the baking sheet and brush them with the egg.

Bake the pretzels for 15 minutes, checking for doneness after the 12 minute mark. Since these pretzels are naturally dark in color, they scorch easily. Let the pretzels cool on the baking sheet for 5 to 10 minutes. Drizzle with frosting before eating.

Raisin Pretzels

1 batch Basic Pretzel dough (page 23)

1 cup raisins or dried cranberries, plumped (see note)

2 teaspoons baking soda

1 cup hot water

1 egg, lightly beaten

Toppings (page 24)

Prepare the pretzel dough as directed in the recipe, adding the raisins as you mix the proofed yeast with the flour.

Place the dough in a bowl sprayed with nonstick cooking spray, cover with plastic wrap, and let it rest overnight in the refrigerator.

Punch the dough down, then turn it out onto a lightly floured work surface and cut it into pieces, depending on the size and type of pretzel you want to make. Follow the directions on pages 18-19 to shape the pretzels. Place the pretzels on a parchment-lined baking sheet, cover them with plastic wrap, and let them rise at room temperature for 45 minutes, or until they have doubled in size.

Preheat the oven to 450°F.

Combine the baking soda and hot water in a bowl. Dip the risen pretzels in the baking soda bath, then return them to the baking sheet and brush them with egg. Sprinkle with the desired toppings.

Bake the pretzels for 15 minutes, or until they are golden brown. Let them cool on the baking sheet for 5 to 10 minutes before eating.

PLUMPING DRIED FRUIT: Measure out the fruit and place it in a bowl. Add enough warm liquid to cover, such as water, fruit juice, or alcohol, depending on the recipe and your tastes. Dark rum and raisins are a good combination. Let the fruit soak for about 10 minutes, or until it is plump and juicy. Drain the liquid before using the fruit in the recipe.

Raisin Bran Pretzels

3½ cups all-purpose flour

1 (¼-ounce) package active
    dry yeast

2 tablespoons sugar

1 teaspoon salt

1½ cups warm water
    (100 to 115°F)

1 cup 100% bran

1 tablespoon butter, softened

½ cup raisins, plumped (see
    note on previous page)

2 teaspoons baking soda

1 cup hot water

1 egg, lightly beaten

Toppings (page 24)

In a large bowl, combine 1½ cups of the flour, the yeast, sugar, and salt.

In a small bowl, combine the warm water, bran, and butter. Add the bran mixture and raisins to the dry ingredients and stir to incorporate. Add the remaining flour, ½ cup at a time, and stir until you have a soft dough.

Punch the dough down, then turn it out onto a lightly floured work surface and knead until it is smooth and elastic, about 5 minutes. If the dough is too sticky, add more flour, 1 teaspoon at a time.

Cover the dough with plastic wrap of a clean kitchen towel and let it rest for 10 minutes.

Cut the dough into pieces, depending on the size and type of pretzel you want to make. Follow the directions on pages 18-19 to shape the pretzels. Place them on parchment-lined baking sheets, cover them with plastic wrap, and let them rise at room temperature for 45 minutes, or until they double in size.

Preheat the oven to 450°F.

Combine the baking soda and hot water in a bowl. Dip the risen pretzels in the baking soda bath, then return them to the baking sheet and brush them with egg. Sprinkle with the desired toppings.

Bake the pretzels for 15 minutes, or until they are golden brown. Let them cool on the baking sheet for 5 to 10 minutes before eating.

Beer Nut Pretzels

1 batch Basic Pretzel dough (page 23)

¾ cups crushed Beer Nuts

2 teaspoons baking soda

1 cup hot water

1 egg, lightly beaten

Toppings (page 24)

Prepare the pretzel dough as directed in the recipe, adding half of the crushed Beer Nuts as you mix the proofed yeast with the flour.

Place the dough in a bowl sprayed with nonstick cooking spray, cover with plastic wrap, and let it rest overnight in the refrigerator.

Punch the dough down, then turn it out onto a lightly floured work surface and cut it into pieces, depending on the size and type of pretzel you want to make. Follow the directions on pages 18-19 to shape the pretzels. Place the pretzels on a parchment-lined baking sheet, cover them with plastic wrap, and let them rise at room temperature for 45 minutes, or until they have doubled in size.

Preheat the oven to 450°F.

Combine the baking soda and hot water in a bowl. Dip the risen pretzels in the baking soda bath, then return them to the baking sheet and brush them with egg. Sprinkle with the remaining Beer Nuts.

Bake the pretzels for 15 minutes, or until they are golden brown. Let them cool on the baking sheet for 5 to 10 minutes before eating.

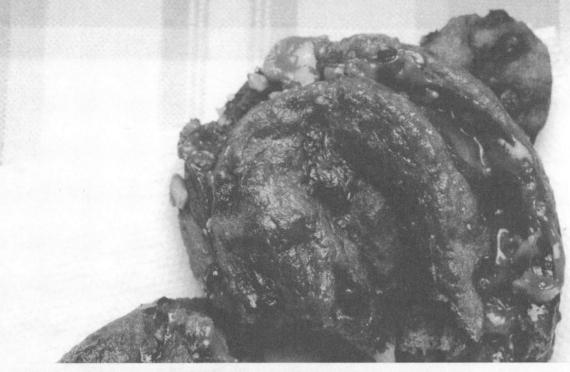

SWEET FILLED PRETZELS

Chocolate-Almond Pretzels

PRETZELS

1 tablespoon active dry yeast

1 cup warm water (100 to 115°F), plus more if needed

¼ cup light brown sugar

3¼ cups all-purpose flour

¼ cup Dutch-processed cocoa

2 teaspoons salt

2 tablespoons sugar

1 teaspoon vanilla extract

1½ cups chocolate chips, milk or semisweet

2 teaspoons baking soda

1 cup hot water

1 egg, lightly beaten

Frosting (page 40), optional

FILLING

8 ounces almond paste

½ cup minced blanched almonds

½ cup confectioners' sugar

1 large egg white

1 teaspoon almond extract

1 teaspoon vanilla extract

In a large mixing bowl, combine the yeast, water, and brown sugar (see Proofing Yeast on page 23). Stir until well incorporated.

Add the flour, cocoa, salt, sugar, and vanilla, and mix until the mixture forms a smooth dough. Stir in the chocolate chips. Place the dough in a bowl sprayed with nonstick cooking spray, cover with plastic wrap, and let it rest overnight in the refrigerator.

To make the filling, combine all the filling ingredients in the bowl of a food processor and process until well mixed. Set aside.

Punch the dough down, then turn it out onto a lightly floured work surface and cut it into 6 pieces. Use your hands to roll the dough into ropes that are about 24 inches long and 2 inches thick. With a rolling pin or buttered hands, flatten the ropes to a 2-inch width each rope.

Spoon the filling into a piping bag with a wide tip (or a ziplock with a corner cut off) and carefully pipe filling down the center of the flattened dough, leaving a ¼-inch border on all sides. Carefully wrap the dough around the filling and pinch it together to seal. Follow the directions on pages 18–19 to shape the pretzels.

Place the pretzels on a parchment-lined baking sheet, cover them with plastic wrap, and let them rise at room temperature for 45 minutes, or until they have doubled in size.

Preheat the oven to 450°F.

Combine the baking soda and hot water in a bowl. Dip the risen pretzels in the baking soda bath, then return them to the baking sheet and brush them with egg.

Bake the pretzels for 15 minutes, checking for doneness after the 12 minute mark. Since these pretzels are naturally dark in color, they scorch easily. Let the pretzels cool on the baking sheet for 5 to 10 minutes. Drizzle with frosting before eating.

Chocolate-Orange Pretzels

PRETZELS

1 tablespoon active dry yeast

1 cup warm water (100 to 115°F), plus more if needed

¼ cup light brown sugar

3¼ cups all-purpose flour

¼ cup Dutch-processed cocoa

2 teaspoons salt

1 teaspoon vanilla extract

2 tablespoons sugar

1½ cups chocolate chips, milk or semisweet, regular sized or mini

4 tablespoons orange marmalade, heated, optional

2 teaspoons baking soda

1 cup hot water

1 egg, lightly beaten

Frosting (page 40), optional

In a large mixing bowl, combine the yeast, water, and 1 tablespoon brown sugar (see Proofing Yeast on page 23).

Add the remaining brown sugar and mix until well incorporated.

Add the flour, cocoa, salt, vanilla, and sugar, and mix until the mixture forms a smooth dough. Stir in the chocolate chips. Place the dough in a bowl sprayed with nonstick cooking spray, cover with plastic wrap, and let it rest overnight in the refrigerator.

Punch the dough down, then turn it out onto a lightly floured work surface and cut it into 6 pieces. Use your hands to roll the dough into ropes that are about 24 inches long and 2 inches thick.

Using a rolling pin or greased hands, flatten the ropes to a 2-inch width. Spread a layer of marmalade on the flattened dough, leaving a ¼-inch border on all sides.

To make the filling, combine the cream cheese, confectioners' sugar, cornstarch, orange zest, orange extract, and milk in a large bowl and mix with an electric mixer for 5 minutes on medium speed, until thoroughly incorporated and smooth. If the mixture is too thick, add a few teaspoons of milk. It should be creamy and smooth.

Spoon the filling into a piping bag with a wide tip (or a ziplock with a corner cut off) and carefully pipe filling down the center of the flattened dough, leaving a ¼-inch border on all sides. Carefully wrap the dough around the filling and pinch it together to seal. Follow the directions on pages 18–19 to shape the pretzels.

Place the pretzels on a parchment-lined baking sheet, cover with

FILLING

8 ounces cream cheese, softened

¾ cup confectioners' sugar

1 teaspoon cornstarch

2 tablespoons grated orange zest

2 tablespoons orange extract or 2 tablespoons Grand Marnier, Cointreau, or Triple Sec

2 tablespoons milk

plastic wrap, and let rise at room temperature for 45 minutes, or until the pretzels have doubled in size.

Preheat the oven to 450°F.

Combine the baking soda and hot water in a bowl. Dip the risen pretzels in the baking soda bath, then return them to the baking sheet and brush them with egg.

Bake the pretzels for 15 minutes, checking for doneness after the 12 minute mark. Since these pretzels are naturally dark in color, they scorch easily.

Let the pretzels cool on the baking sheet for 5 to 10 minutes. Drizzle with frosting before eating.

NOW THAT'S ONE BIG PRETZEL!

Joe Naccio of Federal Baking in Philadelphia, baked the world's largest recorded pretzel, measuring 5 feet across and weighing in at 40 pounds!

Chocolate-Raspberry and Mint Pretzels

PRETZELS

1 tablespoon active dry yeast

1 cup warm water (100 to 115°F), plus more if needed

¼ cup light brown sugar

3¼ cups all-purpose flour

¼ cup Dutch-processed cocoa

2 teaspoons salt

2 tablespoons sugar

1 teaspoon vanilla extract

1½ cups chocolate chips, milk or semisweet

2 teaspoons baking soda

1 cup hot water

1 egg, lightly beaten

Frosting (page 40), optional

FILLING

1 cup raspberry jam, heated

½ tablespoon minced fresh mint

> **VARIATION:**
> You can use any flavor jam in this recipe.

In a large mixing bowl, combine the yeast, water, and brown sugar (see Proofing Yeast on page 23). Stir until well incorporated.

Add the flour, cocoa, salt, sugar, and vanilla, and mix until the mixture forms a smooth dough. Stir in the chocolate chips. Place the dough in a bowl sprayed with nonstick cooking spray, cover with plastic wrap, and let it rest overnight in the refrigerator.

Punch the dough down, turn it out onto a lightly floured work surface, and cut it into 6 pieces. Use your hands to roll the dough into ropes that are about 24 inches long and 2 inches thick. With a rolling pin or buttered hands, flatten the ropes to a 2-inch width.

Spoon the jam into a piping bag with a wide tip (or a ziplock with a corner cut off) and pipe filling down the center of the dough, leaving a ¼-inch border on all sides. Sprinkle mint onto the jam. Carefully wrap the dough around the filling and pinch it together to seal. Follow the directions on pages 18–19 to shape the pretzels.

Place the pretzels on a parchment-lined baking sheet, cover them with plastic wrap, and let them rise at room temperature for 45 minutes, or until they have doubled in size.

Preheat the oven to 400°F.

Combine the baking soda and hot water in a bowl. Dip the risen pretzels in the baking soda bath, then return them to the baking sheet and brush them with egg.

Bake the pretzels for 15 minutes, checking for doneness after the 12 minute mark. Since these pretzels are naturally dark in color, they scorch easily. Let the pretzels cool on the baking sheet for 5 to 10 minutes. Drizzle with frosting before eating.

Chocolate-Espresso Cream Pretzels

PRETZELS

1 tablespoon active dry yeast

1 cup warm water (100 to 115°F), plus more if needed

¼ cup light brown sugar

3¼ cups all-purpose flour

¼ cup Dutch-processed cocoa

2 teaspoons salt

2 tablespoons sugar

1 teaspoon vanilla extract

1½ cups chocolate chips

2 teaspoons baking soda

1 cup hot water

1 egg, lightly beaten

FILLING

2 tablespoons instant espresso powder

⅓ cup evaporated milk

1 teaspoon vanilla extract

2 tablespoons butter, softened

⅓ cup vegetable shortening, softened

1 cup confectioners' sugar

2 egg yolks

In a large mixing bowl, combine the yeast, water, and brown sugar (see Proofing Yeast on page 23). Stir until well incorporated.

Add the flour, cocoa, salt, sugar, and vanilla, and mix until the mixture forms a smooth dough. Stir in the chocolate chips. Place the dough in a bowl sprayed with nonstick cooking spray, cover with plastic wrap, and let it rest overnight in the refrigerator.

To make the filling, combine the espresso powder, milk, and vanilla in a small bowl. In a large bowl, mix the butter and shortening with an electric mixer until thoroughly combined. Add the confectioners' sugar and stir until combined. Beat in the egg yolks, one at a time, until incorporated. Add the espresso mixture and mix on medium speed until the mixture is smooth and fluffy.

Punch the dough down, then turn it out onto a lightly floured work surface and cut it into 6 pieces. Use your hands to roll the dough into ropes that are about 24 inches long and 2 inches thick. With a rolling pin or buttered hands, flatten the ropes to a 2-inch width.

Spoon the filling into a piping bag with a wide tip (or a ziplock with a corner cut off) and pipe filling down the center of the dough, leaving a ¼-inch border on all sides. Fold the dough over the filling and press it together, forming a seal. Follow the directions on pages 18–19 to shape the pretzels. Place them on a parchment-lined baking sheet, cover with plastic wrap, and let them rise at room temperature for 45 minutes, or until they have doubled in size.

Preheat the oven to 450°F.

Combine the baking soda and hot water in a bowl. Dip the risen pretzels in the baking soda bath, then return them to the baking sheet and brush them with egg. Bake the pretzels for 15 minutes, checking for doneness after the 12 minute mark. Let the pretzels cool on the baking sheet for 5 to 10 minutes before eating.

Chocolate–Irish Cream Pretzels

- -

PRETZELS

1 tablespoon active dry yeast

1 cup warm water (100 to 115°F), plus more if needed

¼ cup light brown sugar

3¼ cups all-purpose flour

¼ cup Dutch-processed cocoa

2 teaspoons salt

2 tablespoons sugar

1 teaspoon vanilla extract

1½ cups chocolate chips

2 teaspoons baking soda

1 cup hot water

1 egg, lightly beaten

Frosting (page 40), optional

In a large mixing bowl, combine the yeast, water, and brown sugar (see Proofing Yeast on page 23). Stir until well incorporated.

Add the flour, cocoa, salt, sugar, and vanilla, and mix until the mixture forms a smooth dough. Stir in the chocolate chips. Place the dough in a bowl sprayed with nonstick cooking spray, cover with plastic wrap, and let it rest overnight in the refrigerator.

To make the filling, mix the butter and shortening in a large bowl with an electric mixer on low speed for 3 minutes, or until thoroughly combined. Add the confectioners' sugar and mix for 2 minutes, until combined. Beat in the egg yolks, one at a time, until incorporated. Add the Irish cream and vanilla and mix on medium speed for 2 minutes, until the mixture is smooth and fluffy.

Punch the dough down, turn it out onto a lightly floured work surface, and cut it into 6 pieces. Use your hands to roll the dough into ropes that are about 24 inches long and 2 inches thick. With a rolling pin or buttered hands, flatten the ropes to a 2-inch width.

Spoon the filling into a piping bag with a wide tip (or a ziplock with a corner cut off), then pipe filling down the center of the dough, leaving a ¼-inch border on all sides. Carefully fold the dough over the filling and press it together, forming a seal. Follow the directions on pages 18–19 to shape the pretzels.

Place the pretzels on a parchment-lined baking sheet, cover them with plastic wrap, and let them rise at room temperature for 45 minutes, or until they have doubled in size.

FILLING

2 tablespoons butter, softened

⅓ cup vegetable shortening, softened

1 cup confectioners' sugar

2 egg yolks

4 tablespoons Irish cream liqueur

1 teaspoon vanilla extract

⅓ cup evaporated milk

Preheat the oven to 450°F.

Combine the baking soda and hot water in a bowl. Dip the risen pretzels in the baking soda bath, then return them to the baking sheet and brush them with egg.

Bake the pretzels for 15 minutes, checking for doneness after the 12 minute mark. Since these pretzels are naturally dark in color, they scorch easily. Let the pretzels cool on the baking sheet for 5 to 10 minutes. Drizzle with frosting, if desired.

- -

THROW AWAY THAT RABBIT'S FOOT!

The pretzel is fabled to bring luck, prosperity, and spiritual wholeness. It sure brings a full tummy!

- -

Chocolate-Peppermint Cream Pretzels

PRETZELS

1 tablespoon active dry yeast

1 cup warm water (100 to 115°F), plus more if needed

¼ cup light brown sugar

3¼ cups all-purpose flour

¼ cup Dutch-processed cocoa

2 teaspoons salt

2 tablespoons sugar

1 teaspoon vanilla extract

1½ cups chocolate chips

2 teaspoons baking soda

1 cup hot water

1 egg, lightly beaten

FILLING

2 tablespoons butter, softened

⅓ cup vegetable shortening, softened

1 cup confectioners' sugar

2 egg yolks

1½ teaspoons peppermint extract

1 teaspoon vanilla extract

⅓ cup evaporated milk

In a large mixing bowl, combine the yeast, water, and brown sugar (see Proofing Yeast on page 23). Stir until well incorporated.

Add the flour, cocoa, salt, sugar, and vanilla, and mix until the mixture forms a smooth dough. Stir in the chocolate chips. Place the dough in a bowl sprayed with nonstick cooking spray, cover with plastic wrap, and let it rest overnight in the refrigerator.

To make the filling, mix the butter and shortening in a large bowl with an electric mixer on low speed for 3 minutes, or until combined. Add the confectioners' sugar and mix for 2 minutes, until combined. Beat in the egg yolks, one at a time, until incorporated. Add the peppermint extract and vanilla and mix on medium speed for 2 minutes, until the mixture is smooth and fluffy.

Punch the dough down, then turn it out onto a lightly floured work surface and cut it into 6 pieces. Use your hands to roll the dough into ropes that are about 24 inches long and 2 inches thick. With a rolling pin or buttered hands, flatten the ropes to a 2-inch width.

Spoon the filling into a piping bag with a wide tip (or a ziplock with a corner cut off), then pipe filling down the center of the dough, leaving a ¼-inch border on all sides. Fold the dough over the filling and press it together, forming a seal. Follow the directions on pages 18–19 to shape the pretzels. Place them on a parchment-lined baking sheet, cover with plastic wrap, and let them rise at room temperature for 45 minutes, or until they have doubled in size.

Preheat the oven to 450°F.

Combine the baking soda and hot water in a bowl. Dip the risen pretzels in the baking soda bath, then return them to the baking sheet and brush them with egg. Bake the pretzels for 15 minutes, checking for doneness after the 12 minute mark. Let the pretzels cool on the baking sheet for 5 to 10 minutes before eating.

Chocolate-Hazelnut Cream Pretzels

PRETZELS

1 tablespoon active dry yeast

1 cup warm water (100 to 115°F), plus more if needed

¼ cup light brown sugar

3¼ cups all-purpose flour

¼ cup Dutch-processed cocoa

2 teaspoons salt

2 tablespoons sugar

1 teaspoon vanilla extract

1½ cups chocolate chips

2 teaspoons baking soda

1 cup hot water

1 egg, lightly beaten

FILLING

2 tablespoons butter, softened

⅓ cup vegetable shortening, softened

1 cup confectioners' sugar

2 egg yolks

2 teaspoons Frangelico or Hazelnut liqueur

1 teaspoon vanilla extract

⅓ cup evaporated milk

In a large mixing bowl, combine the yeast, water, and brown sugar (see Proofing Yeast on page 23). Stir until well incorporated.

Add the flour, cocoa, salt, sugar, and vanilla, and mix until the mixture forms a smooth dough. Stir in the chocolate chips. Place the dough in a bowl sprayed with nonstick cooking spray, cover with plastic wrap, and let it rest overnight in the refrigerator.

To make the filling, mix the butter and shortening in a large bowl with an electric mixer on low speed for 3 minutes, or until combined. Add the confectioners' sugar and mix for 2 minutes, until combined. Beat in the egg yolks, one at a time, until incorporated. Add the Frangelico and vanilla and mix on medium speed for 2 minutes, until the mixture is smooth and fluffy.

Punch the dough down, then turn it out onto a lightly floured work surface and cut it into 6 pieces. Use your hands to roll the dough into ropes that are about 24 inches long and 2 inches thick. With a rolling pin or buttered hands, flatten the ropes to a 2-inch width.

Spoon the filling into a piping bag with a wide tip (or a ziplock with a corner cut off), then pipe filling down the center of the dough, leaving a ¼-inch border on all sides. Fold the dough over the filling and press it together, forming a seal. Follow the directions on pages 18–19 to shape the pretzels. Place them on a parchment-lined baking sheet, cover with plastic wrap, and let them rise at room temperature for 45 minutes, or until they have doubled in size.

Preheat the oven to 450°F.

Combine the baking soda and hot water in a bowl. Dip the risen pretzels in the baking soda bath, then return them to the baking sheet and brush them with egg. Bake the pretzels for 15 minutes, checking for doneness after the 12 minute mark. Let the pretzels cool on the baking sheet for 5 to 10 minutes before eating.

Chocolate-Amaretto Cream Pretzels

PRETZELS

1 tablespoon active dry yeast

1 cup warm water (100 to 115°F), plus more if needed

¼ cup light brown sugar

3½ cups all-purpose flour

¼ cup Dutch-processed cocoa

2 teaspoons salt

2 tablespoons sugar

1 teaspoon vanilla extract

1½ cups chocolate chips

2 teaspoons baking soda

1 cup hot water

1 egg, lightly beaten

FILLING

2 tablespoons butter, softened

½ cup vegetable shortening, softened

1 cup confectioners' sugar

2 egg yolks

2 teaspoons Amaretto liqueur or almond extract

1 teaspoon vanilla extract

⅓ cup evaporated milk

In a large mixing bowl, combine the yeast, water, and brown sugar (see Proofing Yeast on page 23). Stir until well incorporated.

Add the flour, cocoa, salt, sugar, and vanilla, and mix until the mixture forms a smooth dough. Stir in the chocolate chips. Place the dough in a bowl sprayed with nonstick cooking spray, cover with plastic wrap, and let it rest overnight in the refrigerator.

To make the filling, mix the butter and shortening in a large bowl with an electric mixer on low speed for 3 minutes, or until thoroughly combined. Add the confectioners' sugar and mix for 2 minutes, until combined. Beat in the egg yolks, one at a time, until incorporated. Add amaretto and vanilla and mix on medium speed for 2 minutes, until the mixture is smooth and fluffy.

Punch the dough down, then turn it out onto a lightly floured work surface and cut it into 6 pieces. Use your hands to roll the dough into ropes that are about 24 inches long and 2 inches thick. With a rolling pin or buttered hands, flatten the ropes to a 2-inch width.

Spoon the filling into a piping bag with a wide tip (or a ziplock with a corner cut off), then pipe filling down the center of the dough, leaving a ¼-inch border on all sides. Fold the dough over the filling and press it together, forming a seal. Follow the directions on pages 18–19 to shape the pretzels. Place them on a parchment-lined baking sheet, cover with plastic wrap, and let them rise at room temperature for 45 minutes, or until they have doubled in size.

Preheat the oven to 450°F.

Combine the baking soda and hot water in a bowl. Dip the risen pretzels in the baking soda bath, then return them to the baking sheet and brush them with egg. Bake the pretzels for 15 minutes, checking for doneness after the 12 minute mark. Let the pretzels cool on the baking sheet for 5 to 10 minutes before eating.

Choco-Coconut Pretzels

PRETZELS

1 tablespoon active dry yeast

1 cup warm water (100 to 115°F), plus more if needed

¼ cup light brown sugar

3¼ cups all-purpose flour

¼ cup Dutch-processed cocoa

2 teaspoons salt

2 tablespoons sugar

1 teaspoon vanilla extract

1½ cups chocolate chips

2 teaspoons baking soda

1 cup hot water

1 egg, lightly beaten

FILLING

3 tablespoons cornstarch

⅓ cup sugar

⅛ teaspoon salt

1½ cup milk

2 egg yolks

½ cup shredded coconut

¼ cup cream cheese

1 teaspoon vanilla extract

½ teaspoon coconut extract

In a large mixing bowl, combine the yeast, water, and brown sugar (see Proofing Yeast on page 23). Stir until well incorporated.

Add the flour, cocoa, salt, sugar, and vanilla, and mix until the mixture forms a smooth dough. Stir in the chocolate chips. Place the dough in a bowl sprayed with nonstick cooking spray, cover with plastic wrap, and let it rest overnight in the refrigerator.

To make the filling, combine the cornstarch, sugar, salt, milk, and egg yolks in a medium saucepan and stir over medium heat. Cook for 5 minutes, stirring constantly, until the mixture thickens and bubbles. Remove from the heat and stir in the coconut, cream cheese, and extracts. Set aside to cool completely.

Punch the dough down, then turn it out onto a lightly floured work surface and cut it into 6 pieces. Use your hands to roll the dough into ropes that are about 24 inches long and 2 inches thick. With a rolling pin or buttered hands, flatten the ropes to a 2-inch width.

Spoon the filling into a piping bag with a wide tip (or a ziplock with a corner cut off), then pipe filling down the center of the dough, leaving a ¼-inch border on all sides. Fold the dough over the filling and press it together, forming a seal. Follow the directions on pages 18–19 to shape the pretzels.

Place the pretzels on a parchment-lined baking sheet, cover with plastic wrap, and let them rise at room temperature for 45 minutes, or until they have doubled in size.

Preheat the oven to 450°F.

Combine the baking soda and hot water in a bowl. Dip the risen pretzels in the baking soda bath, then return them to the baking sheet and brush them with egg. Bake the pretzels for 15 minutes, checking for doneness after the 12 minute mark. Let the pretzels cool on the baking sheet for 5 to 10 minutes before eating.

"Danish Pastry" Pretzels

Pretzels

1 tablespoon active dry yeast

1 cup warm water (100 to 115°F), plus more if needed

¼ cup light brown sugar

3½ cups all-purpose flour

2 teaspoons salt

2 tablespoons ground cinnamon

2 teaspoons baking soda

1 cup hot water

1 egg, lightly beaten

Filling

7 ounces cream cheese, softened

½ cup confectioners' sugar

1 cup fruit pie filling of your choice

¼ cup chopped walnuts

Topping

¼ cup Bisquick

4 tablespoons butter, softened

¼ cup brown sugar

In a large mixing bowl, combine the yeast, water, and brown sugar (see Proofing Yeast on page 23). Stir until well incorporated.

Add the flour, salt, and cinnamon and stir until the mixture forms a smooth dough. Place the dough in a bowl sprayed with nonstick cooking spray, cover with plastic wrap, and let it rest overnight in the refrigerator.

To make the filling, combine the cream cheese and confectioners' sugar in a large bowl and mix with an electric mixer on high for 3 minutes, or until smooth. In a separate bowl, combine the pie filling and walnuts. Drain, if necessary.

Punch the dough down, then turn it out onto a lightly floured work surface and cut it into 6 pieces. Use your hands to roll the dough into ropes that are about 24 inches long and 2 inches thick. With a rolling pin or buttered hands, flatten the ropes to a 2-inch width.

Spoon the filling into a piping bag with a wide tip (or a ziplock with a corner cut off), then pipe filling down the center of the dough, leaving a ¼-inch border on all sides. Top with the fruit and walnut mixture. Fold the dough over the filling and press it together, forming a seal. Follow the directions on pages 18-19 to shape the pretzels.

Place the pretzels on a parchment-lined baking sheet, cover them with plastic wrap, and let them rise at room temperature for 45 minutes, or until they have doubled in size.

Preheat the oven to 400°F.

In a small bowl, combine the Bisquick, butter, and brown sugar.

Combine the baking soda and hot water in a bowl. Dip the risen pretzels in the baking soda bath, then return them to the baking sheet and brush them with egg. Sprinkle with the Bisquick mixture. Bake the pretzels for 15 minutes, or until they are golden brown. Let them cool on the baking sheet for 5 to 10 minutes before eating.

PB and J Pretzels

PRETZELS

1 batch Basic Pretzel dough
  (page 23)

2 teaspoons baking soda

1 cup hot water

1 egg, lightly beaten

FILLING

1 cup peanut butter, heated

1 cup fruit preserves, heated

Prepare the pretzel dough as directed in the recipe.

Place the dough in a bowl sprayed with nonstick cooking spray, cover with plastic wrap, and let it rest overnight in the refrigerator.

Punch the dough down, then turn it out onto a lightly floured work surface and cut it into 6 pieces. Use your hands to roll the dough into ropes that are about 24 inches long and 2 inches thick. With a rolling pin or buttered hands, flatten the ropes to a 2-inch width.

Spoon the peanut butter and fruit preserves into two separate piping bags with wide tips (or ziplock bags with a corner cut off). Pipe peanut butter down the center of the dough, leaving a ¼-inch border on all sides. Pipe preserves alongside the peanut butter, maintaining the border on all sides. Fold the dough over the filling and press it together, forming a seal. Follow the directions on pages 18-19 to shape the pretzels.

Place the pretzels on a parchment-lined baking sheet, cover them with plastic wrap, and let them rise at room temperature for 45 minutes, or until they have doubled in size.

Preheat the oven to 400°F.

Combine the baking soda and hot water in a bowl. Dip the risen pretzels in the baking soda bath, then return them to the baking sheet and brush them with egg.

Bake the pretzels for 12 minutes, or until they are golden brown. Let them cool on the baking sheet for 5 to 10 minutes before eating.

Peanut Butter and Marshmallow Pretzel Bites

PRETZELS

1 batch Basic Pretzel dough
  (page 23)

2 teaspoons baking soda

1 cup hot water

1 egg, lightly beaten

FILLING

1 cup peanut butter, smooth or
  crunchy, heated

1 cup Marshmallow Fluff, heated

Prepare the pretzel dough as directed in the recipe.

Place the dough in a bowl sprayed with nonstick cooking spray, cover with plastic wrap, and let it rest overnight in the refrigerator.

Punch the dough down, then turn it out onto a lightly floured work surface and cut it into 6 pieces. Use your hands to roll the dough into ropes that are about 24 inches long and 2 inches thick. With a rolling pin or buttered hands, flatten the ropes to a 2-inch width.

Spoon the peanut butter and Marshmallow Fluff into two separate piping bags with wide tips (or ziplock bags with a corner cut off). Pipe peanut butter down the center of the dough, leaving a 1/4-inch border on all sides. Pipe Fluff alongside the peanut butter, maintaining the border on all sides. Fold the dough over the filling and press it together, forming a seal. Follow the directions on pages 18–19 to shape the pretzels.

Place the pretzels on a parchment-lined baking sheet, cover them with plastic wrap, and let them rise at room temperature for 45 minutes, or until they have doubled in size.

Preheat the oven to 400°F.

Combine the baking soda and hot water in a bowl. Dip the risen pretzels in the baking soda bath, then return them to the baking sheet and brush them with egg.

Bake the pretzels for 12 minutes, or until they are golden brown. Let them cool on the baking sheet for 5 to 10 minutes before eating.

VARIATION: Make these into Chocolate Peanut Butter and Marshmallow Bites by using the dough from the Chocolate Pretzels on page 40.

Salty Chocolate-Caramel Pretzels

PRETZELS

1 tablespoon active dry yeast

1 cup warm water (100 to 115°F), plus more if needed

¼ cup light brown sugar

3¼ cups all-purpose flour

¼ cup Dutch-processed cocoa

2 teaspoons salt

2 tablespoons sugar

1 teaspoon vanilla extract

1½ cups chocolate chips, milk or semisweet

2 teaspoons baking soda

1 cup hot water

1 egg, lightly beaten

Frosting (page 40), optional

FILLING

1 cup chopped caramel candies

1 cup mini chocolate chips

2 tablespoons kosher salt

In a large mixing bowl, combine the yeast, water, and brown sugar (see Proofing Yeast on page 23). Stir until well incorporated.

Add the flour, cocoa, salt, sugar, and vanilla, and mix until the mixture forms a smooth dough. Stir in the chocolate chips. Place the dough in a bowl sprayed with nonstick cooking spray, cover with plastic wrap, and let it rest overnight in the refrigerator.

Combine the caramels and chocolate chips in a medium-sized bowl.

Punch the dough down, then turn it out onto a lightly floured work surface and cut it into 6 pieces. Use your hands to roll the dough into ropes that are about 24 inches long and 2 inches thick. With a rolling pin or buttered hands, flatten the ropes to a 2-inch width, then top each with the caramel-chocolate mixture, leaving a ¼-inch border on all sides. Sprinkle with salt and fold the dough over the filling, pressing it together to form a seal. Follow the directions on pages 18-19 to shape the pretzels.

Place the pretzels on a parchment-lined baking sheet, cover them with plastic wrap, and let them rise at room temperature for 45 minutes, or until they have doubled in size.

Preheat the oven to 400°F.

Combine the baking soda and hot water in a bowl. Dip the risen pretzels in the baking soda bath, then return them to the baking sheet and brush them with egg.

Bake the pretzels for 15 minutes, checking for doneness after the 12 minute mark. Since these pretzels are naturally dark in color, they scorch easily. Let the pretzels cool on the baking sheet for 5 to 10 minutes. Drizzle with frosting before eating.

Pecan Pie Pretzels

- -

PRETZELS

1 batch Basic Pretzel dough
(page 23)

2 teaspoons baking soda

1 cup hot water

1 egg, lightly beaten

FILLING

2 tablespoons unsalted butter

¼ cup packed light brown sugar

¾ cup light corn syrup

2 tablespoons vanilla extract

½ cup chopped pecans, toasted

1 egg, lightly beaten

Prepare the pretzel dough as directed in the recipe.

Place the dough in a bowl sprayed with nonstick cooking spray, cover with plastic wrap, and let it rest overnight in the refrigerator.

To make the filling, combine the butter, brown sugar, and corn syrup in a medium-sized saucepan set over medium heat. Bring to a boil, stirring constantly. Boil for 1 minute, then remove the pan from the heat and stir in the vanilla and pecans. Set aside to cool for 10 minutes, then whisk in the egg and set aside.

Punch the dough down, then turn it out onto a lightly floured work surface and cut it into 6 pieces. Use your hands to roll the dough into ropes that are about 24 inches long and 2 inches thick. With a rolling pin or buttered hands, flatten the ropes to a 2-inch width.

Spoon the filling into a piping bag with a wide tip (or a ziplock with a corner cut off), then pipe filling down the center of the dough, leaving a ¼-inch border on all sides. Fold the dough over the filling and press it together, forming a seal. Follow the directions on pages 18-19 to shape the pretzels. Place them on a parchment-lined baking sheet, cover with plastic wrap, and let them rise at room temperature for 45 minutes, or until they have doubled in size.

Preheat the oven to 400°F.

Combine the baking soda and hot water in a bowl. Dip the risen pretzels in the baking soda bath, then return them to the baking sheet and brush them with egg.

Bake the pretzels for 10 minutes, or until they are golden brown. Let them cool on the baking sheet for 5 to 10 minutes before eating.

Marmy's Turtle Pretzels

PRETZELS

1 tablespoon active dry yeast

1 cup warm water (100 to
    115°F), plus more if needed

¼ cup light brown sugar

3¼ cups all-purpose flour

¼ cup Dutch-processed cocoa

2 teaspoons salt

2 tablespoons sugar

1 teaspoon vanilla extract

1½ cups chocolate chips

2 teaspoons baking soda

1 cup hot water

1 egg, lightly beaten

Frosting (page 40), optional

FILLING

½ cup chocolate chips

½ cup chopped pecans

½ cup chopped caramel
    candies

In a large mixing bowl, combine the yeast, water, and brown sugar (see Proofing Yeast on page 23). Stir until well incorporated.

Add the flour, cocoa, salt, sugar, and vanilla, and mix until the mixture forms a smooth dough. Stir in the chocolate chips. Place the dough in a bowl sprayed with nonstick cooking spray, cover with plastic wrap, and let it rest overnight in the refrigerator.

To make the filling, combine the chocolate chips, pecans, and caramels in a medium-sized bowl.

Punch the dough down, then turn it out onto a lightly floured work surface and cut it into 6 pieces. Use your hands to roll the dough into ropes that are about 24 inches long and 2 inches thick. With a rolling pin or buttered hands, flatten the ropes to a 2-inch width, then top each with about 2 tablespoons of the filling, leaving a ¼-inch border on all sides. Fold the dough over the filling and press it together, forming a seal around the cheese. Follow the directions on pages 18–19 to shape the pretzels.

Place the pretzels on a parchment-lined baking sheet, cover them with plastic wrap, and let them rise at room temperature for 45 minutes, or until they have doubled in size.

Preheat the oven to 450°F.

Combine the baking soda and hot water in a bowl. Dip the risen pretzels in the baking soda bath, then return them to the baking sheet and brush them with egg.

Bake the pretzels for 15 minutes, checking for doneness after the 12 minute mark. Let the pretzels cool on the baking sheet for 5 to 10 minutes. Drizzle with frosting before eating.

Blueberry Pretzels

PRETZELS

1 tablespoon active dry yeast

1 cup warm water (100 to 115°F), plus more if needed

¼ cup light brown sugar

3½ cups all-purpose flour

2 teaspoons salt

5 tablespoons ground cinnamon

2 teaspoons baking soda

1 cup hot water

1 egg, lightly beaten

FILLING

1 cup blueberry pie filling, heated

¼ cup sugar

In a large mixing bowl, combine the yeast, water, and brown sugar (see Proofing Yeast on page 23). Stir until well incorporated.

Add the flour, salt, and 2 tablespoons of the cinnamon and mix until the mixture forms a smooth dough. Place the dough in a bowl sprayed with nonstick cooking spray, cover with plastic wrap, and let it rest overnight in the refrigerator.

Punch the dough down, then turn it out onto a lightly floured work surface and cut it into 6 pieces. Use your hands to roll the dough into ropes that are about 24 inches long and 2 inches thick. With a rolling pin or buttered hands, flatten the ropes to a 2-inch width, then top each with about 2 tablespoons of the blueberry filling, leaving a ¼-inch border on all sides. Fold the dough over the filling and press it together, forming a seal. Follow the directions on pages 18–19 to shape the pretzels.

Place the pretzels on a parchment-lined baking sheet, cover them with plastic wrap, and let them rise at room temperature for 45 minutes, or until they have doubled in size.

Preheat the oven to 450°F.

Combine the sugar with the remaining 3 tablespoons cinnamon.

Combine the baking soda and hot water in a bowl. Dip the risen pretzels in the baking soda bath, then return them to the baking sheet and brush them with egg. Sprinkle with the cinnamon sugar.

Bake the pretzels for 15 minutes, or until they are golden brown. Let them cool on the baking sheet for 5 to 10 minutes before eating.

Gigi's Caramel Apple Pretzels

PRETZELS

1 batch Basic Pretzel dough
(page 23)

2 teaspoons baking soda

1 cup hot water

1 egg, lightly beaten

Raw sugar, for topping

Ground cinnamon, for topping

Caramel Pretzel Dip, optional
(page 168)

FILLING

1 Granny Smith apple, peeled,
cored, and diced

1 cup chopped caramel
candies

Prepare the pretzel dough as directed in the recipe.

Place the dough in a bowl sprayed with nonstick cooking spray, cover with plastic wrap, and let it rest overnight in the refrigerator.

Punch the dough down, then turn it out onto a lightly floured work surface and cut it into 6 pieces. Use your hands to roll the dough into ropes that are about 24 inches long and 2 inches thick. With a rolling pin or buttered hands, flatten the ropes to a 2-inch width, then top each with the apples and caramels, leaving a ¼-inch border on all sides. Fold the dough over the filling and press it together, forming a seal. Follow the directions on pages 18–19 to shape the pretzels.

Place the pretzels on a parchment-lined baking sheet, cover them with plastic wrap, and let them rise at room temperature for 45 minutes, or until they have doubled in size.

Preheat the oven to 400°F.

Combine the baking soda and hot water in a bowl. Dip the risen pretzels in the baking soda bath, then return them to the baking sheet and brush them with egg. Sprinkle with raw sugar, cinnamon, or both.

Bake the pretzels for 10 minutes, or until they are golden brown. Let them cool on the baking sheet for 5 to 10 minutes before eating. Serve with Caramel Pretzel Dip.

Apple Cobbler Pretzels

PRETZELS

1 batch Basic Pretzel dough
  (page 23)

2 teaspoons baking soda

1 cup hot water

1 egg, lightly beaten

Raw sugar, for topping

Ground cinnamon, for topping

FILLING

1 cup apple pie filling, heated

¼ cup quick-cooking rolled oats

3 tablespoons butter

¼ cup brown sugar

1 teaspoon cinnamon

½ teaspoon nutmeg

Prepare the pretzel dough as directed in the recipe.

Place the dough in a bowl sprayed with nonstick cooking spray, cover with plastic wrap, and let it rest overnight in the refrigerator.

Heat the apple filling in a saucepan over medium-low heat. Add the oats, butter, sugar, cinnamon, and nutmeg and stir to combine. Cook until warmed through, about 10 minutes. Set aside to cool to room temperature.

Punch the dough down, then turn it out onto a lightly floured work surface and cut it into 6 pieces. Use your hands to roll the dough into ropes that are about 24 inches long and 2 inches thick. With a rolling pin or buttered hands, flatten the ropes to a 2-inch width, then top each with about 2 tablespoons of apple filling, leaving a ¼-inch border on all sides. Fold the dough over the filling and press it together, forming a seal. Follow the directions on pages 18-19 to shape the pretzels.

Place the pretzels on a parchment-lined baking sheet, cover them with plastic wrap, and let them rise at room temperature for 45 minutes, or until they have doubled in size.

Preheat the oven to 375°F.

Combine the baking soda and hot water in a bowl. Dip the risen pretzels in the baking soda bath, then return them to the baking sheet and brush them with egg. Sprinkle with raw sugar and cinnamon.

Bake the pretzels for 10 minutes, or until they are golden brown. Let them cool on the baking sheet for 5 to 10 minutes before eating.

Strawberry Pretzels

PRETZELS

1 batch Basic Pretzel dough
(page 23)

2 teaspoons baking soda

1 cup hot water

1 egg, lightly beaten

FILLING

1 cup strawberry jam, heated

Prepare the pretzel dough as directed in the recipe.

Place the dough in a bowl sprayed with nonstick cooking spray, cover with plastic wrap, and let it rest overnight in the refrigerator.

Punch the dough down, then turn it out onto a lightly floured work surface and cut it into 6 pieces. Use your hands to roll the dough into ropes that are about 24 inches long and 2 inches thick. With a rolling pin or buttered hands, flatten the ropes to a 2-inch width.

Spoon the jam into a piping bag with a wide tip (or a ziplock with a corner cut off), then pipe filling down the center of the dough, leaving a ¼-inch border on all sides. Fold the dough over the filling and press it together, forming a seal. Follow the directions on pages 18–19 to shape the pretzels.

Place the pretzels on a parchment-lined baking sheet, cover them with plastic wrap, and let them rise at room temperature for 45 minutes, or until they have doubled in size.

Preheat the oven to 400°F.

Combine the baking soda and hot water in a bowl. Dip the risen pretzels in the baking soda bath, then return them to the baking sheet and brush them with egg.

Bake the pretzels for 10 minutes, or until they are golden brown. Let them cool on the baking sheet for 5 to 10 minutes before eating.

VARIATION: You can use any flavor jam in this recipe. Make one of every kind!

Pear, Port, and Walnut Pretzels

PRETZELS

1 batch Basic Pretzel dough
  (page 23)

2 teaspoons baking soda

1 cup hot water

1 egg, lightly beaten

FILLING

¼ cup port wine

¼ cup sugar

2 pears, cored and diced

Pinch of ground clove

Pinch of ground cinnamon

1 teaspoon vanilla extract

¼ cup chopped walnuts

Prepare the pretzel dough as directed in the recipe.

Place the dough in a bowl sprayed with nonstick cooking spray, cover with plastic wrap, and let it rest overnight in the refrigerator.

To make the filling, heat the port and sugar in a large pan over medium heat for 5 minutes, mixing until the sugar dissolves. Raise the heat and bring the mixture to a gentle boil. Add the pears, clove, and cinnamon. Lower the heat and simmer for 10 minutes, or until the liquid becomes syrupy and the pears soften. Remove the pan from the heat and stir in the vanilla and walnuts. Set aside to cool completely.

Punch the dough down, then turn it out onto a lightly floured work surface and cut it into 6 pieces. Use your hands to roll the dough into ropes that are about 24 inches long and 2 inches thick. With a rolling pin or buttered hands, flatten the ropes to a 2-inch width. Carefully spoon the pear filling into the center of the flattened dough, leaving a ¼-inch border on all sides. Fold the dough over to encase the filling, and press it together, forming a seal. Follow the directions on pages 18–19 to shape the pretzels.

Place the pretzels on a parchment-lined baking sheet, cover them with plastic wrap, and let them rise at room temperature for 45 minutes, or until they have doubled in size.

Preheat the oven to 450°F.

Combine the baking soda and hot water in a bowl. Dip the risen pretzels in the baking soda bath, then return them to the baking sheet and brush them with egg.

Bake the pretzels for 15 minutes, or until they are golden brown. Let them cool on the baking sheet for 5 to 10 minutes before eating.

WHAT A HAPPY ACCIDENT!

Fans of the hard pretzel will be happy to know that, much like sourdough bread, the hard pretzel was the result of an accident.

It is said that in medieval Europe, a young baker fell asleep while preparing his soft pretzels. When he awoke, the result was a darker hard pretzel. Fortunately for him, his boss loved it. Back in those days, folks were routinely guillotined for the most minor of infractions!

SAVORY FILLED PRETZELS

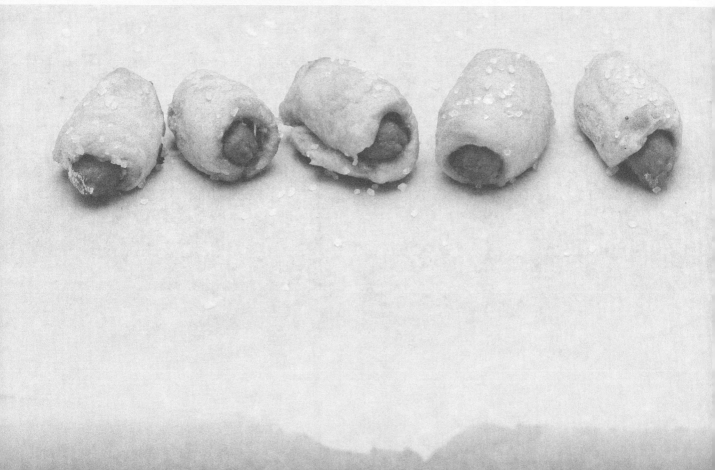

Cheesy Pretzel Bites

PRETZELS

1 batch Basic Pretzel dough
    (page 23)

2 teaspoons baking soda

1 cup hot water

1 egg, lightly beaten

Toppings (page 24)

FILLING

2 packages dry cheese from
    packaged macaroni and
    cheese

¼ cup milk

7 ounces cream cheese,
    softened

Prepare the pretzel dough as directed in the recipe.

Place the dough in a bowl sprayed with nonstick cooking spray, cover with plastic wrap, and let it rest overnight in the refrigerator.

To make the filling, combine the dry cheese, milk, and cream cheese. Stir until it is a smooth consistency. Set aside.

Punch the dough down, then turn it out onto a lightly floured work surface and cut it into 12 pieces. Roll each piece out to a 18- to 24-inch-long rope, about 1 inch thick. With a rolling pin or buttered hands, flatten the ropes to a 2-inch width.

Spoon the filling into a piping bag with a wide tip (or a ziplock with a corner cut off) and pipe along the center of each dough rope, leaving a ¼-inch border on all sides. Fold the dough over the filling and press it together, forming a seal.

Carefully cut the ropes into 1-inch pieces. Place the pretzel bites on a parchment-lined baking sheet, cover them with plastic wrap, and let them rise at room temperature for 45 minutes, or until they have doubled in size.

Preheat the oven to 400°F.

Combine the baking soda and hot water in a bowl. Dip the risen pretzel bitess in the baking soda bath, then return them to the baking sheet and brush them with egg. Sprinkle with the desired toppings.

Bake the pretzel bitess for 15 to 20 minutes, or until they are golden brown. Let them cool on the baking sheet for 5 to 10 minutes before eating.

Honey Mustard Pretzels

PRETZELS

1 batch Basic Pretzel dough
(page 23)

2 teaspoons baking soda

1 cup hot water

1 egg, lightly beaten

Toppings (page 24)

FILLING

¾ cup honey mustard

Prepare the pretzel dough as directed in the recipe.

Place the dough in a bowl sprayed with nonstick cooking spray, cover with plastic wrap, and let it rest overnight in the refrigerator.

Punch the dough down, then turn it out onto a lightly floured work surface and cut it into 6 pieces. Use your hands to roll the dough into ropes that are about 24 inches long and 2 inches thick. With a rolling pin or buttered hands, flatten the ropes to a 2-inch width.

Spoon the honey mustard into a piping bag with a wide tip (or a ziplock with a corner cut off) and pipe along the center of each dough rope, leaving a ¼ inch border on all sides. Fold the dough over the filling and press it together, forming a seal. Follow the directions on pages 18-19 to shape the pretzels.

Place the pretzels on a parchment-lined baking sheet, cover them with plastic wrap, and let them rise at room temperature for 45 minutes, or until they have doubled in size.

Preheat the oven to 400°F.

Combine the baking soda and hot water in a bowl. Dip the risen pretzels in the baking soda bath, then return them to the baking sheet and brush them with egg. Sprinkle with the desired toppings.

Bake the pretzels for 15 minutes, or until they are golden brown. Let them cool on the baking sheet for 5 to 10 minutes before eating.

Pretzel Dogs

PRETZELS

1 batch Basic Pretzel dough
(page 23)

2 teaspoons baking soda

1 cup hot water

1 egg, lightly beaten

Toppings (page 24)

Honey Mustard Pretzel Dip
(page 162) or plain mustard,
for dipping

FILLING

4 all-beef hotdogs, diced
for larger pretzels, cut into
bite-sized pieces for bites

½ cup plain or honey mustard

Prepare the pretzel dough as directed in the recipe.

Place the dough in a bowl sprayed with nonstick cooking spray, cover with plastic wrap, and let it rest overnight in the refrigerator.

Punch the dough down, then turn it out onto a lightly floured work surface and cut it into 6 pieces. Use your hands to roll the dough into ropes that are about 24 inches long and 2 inches thick. With a rolling pin or buttered hands, flatten the ropes to a 2-inch width, then top with hot dog pieces, leaving a ¼-inch border on all sides. Spoon the mustard into a piping bag with a wide tip (or a ziplock with a corner cut off) and pipe along the center of each dough rope. Fold the dough over the fillings and press it together, forming a seal. Follow the directions on pages 18-19 to shape the pretzels.

Place the pretzels on a parchment-lined baking sheet, cover them with plastic wrap, and let them rise at room temperature for 45 minutes, or until they have doubled in size.

Preheat the oven to 400°F.

Combine the baking soda and hot water in a bowl. Dip the risen pretzels in the baking soda bath, then return them to the baking sheet and brush them with egg. Sprinkle with the desired toppings.

Bake the pretzels for 15 minutes, or until they are golden brown. Let them cool on the baking sheet for 5 to 10 minutes before eating with mustard.

Bratwurst, Mustard, and Sauerkraut Pretzels

PRETZELS

1 batch Basic Pretzel dough
  (page 23)

2 teaspoons baking soda

1 cup hot water

1 egg, lightly beaten

Toppings (page 24)

FILLING

1 (12-ounce) can beer

2 bratwurst sausages, diced

1 tablespoon olive oil

1 cup diced onion

½ teaspoon caraway seeds

½ cup sauerkraut, drained

Prepare the pretzel dough as directed in the recipe.

Place the dough in a bowl sprayed with nonstick cooking spray, cover with plastic wrap, and let it rest overnight in the refrigerator.

To make the filling, heat the beer in a large skillet over medium heat. Add the bratwurst and bring the beer to a simmer. Lower the heat, cover, and let the bratwurst simmer for 5 minutes.

Heat the olive oil in a medium-sized skillet. Add the onions and caraway seeds and cook for 7 minutes, until the onions are soft. Remove from the heat, stir in the sauerkraut, and bratwurst. Set aside to cool completely.

Punch the dough down, then turn it out onto a lightly floured work surface and cut it into 6 pieces. Use your hands to roll the dough into ropes that are about 24 inches long and 2 inches thick. With a rolling pin or buttered hands, flatten the ropes to a 2-inch width. Carefully spoon the filling into the center of each flattened rope, leaving a ¼-inch border on all sides. Fold the dough over the filling and press it together, forming a seal. Follow the directions on pages 18–19 to shape the pretzels.

Place the pretzels on a parchment-lined baking sheet, cover them with plastic wrap, and let them rise at room temperature for 45 minutes, or until they have doubled in size.

Preheat the oven to 400°F.

Combine the baking soda and hot water in a bowl. Dip the risen pretzels in the baking soda bath, then return them to the baking sheet and brush them with egg. Sprinkle with the desired toppings.

Bake the pretzels for 15 minutes, or until they are golden brown. Let them cool on the baking sheet for 5 to 10 minutes before eating.

Garlic and Onion Pretzels

PRETZELS

1 batch Basic Pretzel dough
(page 23)

2 teaspoons baking soda

1 cup hot water

1 egg, lightly beaten

Toppings (page 24)

FILLING

3 tablespoons extra-virgin
olive oil

1½ cups diced onions

3 garlic cloves, minced

1 teaspoon kosher salt

Pepper

¼ teaspoon dried marjoram or
1 teaspoon fresh

¼ teaspoon dried thyme or
1 teaspoon fresh

Prepare the pretzel dough as directed in the recipe.

Place the dough in a bowl sprayed with nonstick cooking spray, cover with plastic wrap, and let it rest overnight in the refrigerator.

To make the filling, heat the olive oil in a large skillet over medium heat. Add the onions and garlic and stir to coat. Add the salt, pepper to taste, marjoram, and thyme, and cook for 7 minutes, until the onions and garlic are soft. Taste and adjust the seasonings, if necessary. Set aside to cool.

Punch the dough down, then turn it out onto a lightly floured work surface and cut it into 6 pieces. Use your hands to roll the dough into ropes that are about 24 inches long and 2 inches thick. With a rolling pin or buttered hands, flatten the ropes to a 2-inch width. Carefully spoon the filling into the center of each flattened rope, leaving a ¼-inch border on all sides. Fold the dough over the filling and press it together, forming a seal. Follow the directions on pages 18-19 to shape the pretzels.

Place the pretzels on a parchment-lined baking sheet, cover them with plastic wrap, and let them rise at room temperature for 45 minutes, or until they have doubled in size.

Preheat the oven to 400°F.

Combine the baking soda and hot water in a bowl. Dip the risen pretzels in the baking soda bath, then return them to the baking sheet and brush them with egg. Sprinkle with any remaining filling or other desired toppings.

Bake the pretzels for 15 minutes, or until they are golden brown. Let them cool on the baking sheet for 5 to 10 minutes before eating.

Cheddar Cheese Pretzels

PRETZELS

1 batch Basic Pretzel dough
(page 23)

2 teaspoons baking soda

1 cup hot water

1 egg, lightly beaten

Toppings (page 24)

FILLING

1 cup shredded cheddar cheese

Prepare the pretzel dough as directed in the recipe.

Place the dough in a bowl sprayed with nonstick cooking spray, cover with plastic wrap, and let it rest overnight in the refrigerator.

Punch the dough down, then turn it out onto a lightly floured work surface and cut it into 6 pieces. Use your hands to roll the dough into ropes that are about 24 inches long and 2 inches thick. With a rolling pin or buttered hands, flatten the ropes to a 2-inch width. Carefully spoon the cheese into the center of each flattened rope, leaving a ¼-inch border on all sides. Fold the dough over the filling and press it together, forming a seal. Follow the directions on pages 18-19 to shape the pretzels.

Place the pretzels on a parchment-lined baking sheet, cover them with plastic wrap, and let them rise at room temperature for 45 minutes, or until they have doubled in size.

Preheat the oven to 400°F.

Combine the baking soda and hot water in a bowl. Dip the risen pretzels in the baking soda bath, then return them to the baking sheet and brush them with egg. Sprinkle with the desired toppings.

Bake the pretzels for 12 minutes, or until they are golden brown. Let them cool on the baking sheet for 5 to 10 minutes before eating.

Tomato, Basil, and Cheese Pretzels

PRETZELS

1 batch Basic Pretzel dough
(page 23)

2 teaspoons baking soda

1 cup hot water

1 egg, lightly beaten

FILLING

½ pint cherry or grape
tomatoes, cut into
small pieces

½ cup basil, minced

1 cup shredded
mozzarella cheese

Prepare the pretzel dough as directed in the recipe.

Place the dough in a bowl sprayed with nonstick cooking spray, cover with plastic wrap, and let it rest overnight in the refrigerator.

Punch the dough down, then turn it out onto a lightly floured work surface and cut it into 6 pieces. Use your hands to roll the dough into ropes that are about 24 inches long and 2 inches thick. Follow the directions on pages 18–19 to shape the pretzels.

Place the pretzels on a parchment-lined baking sheet, cover them with plastic wrap, and let them rise at room temperature for 45 minutes, or until they have doubled in size.

Preheat the oven to 400°F.

Combine the baking soda and hot water in a bowl. Dip the risen pretzels in the baking soda bath, then return them to the baking sheet and brush them with egg.

Carefully push the tomatoes into the dough and sprinkle the pretzels with basil and mozzarella cheese.

Bake the pretzels for 12 minutes, or until they are golden brown. Let them cool on the baking sheet for 5 to 10 minutes before eating.

Pesto Pretzel

PRETZELS

1 batch Basic Pretzel dough (page 23)

2 teaspoons baking soda

1 cup hot water

1 egg, lightly beaten

Toppings (page 24)

FILLING

2 cups basil leaves

½ cup extra-virgin olive oil

4 garlic cloves

¼ cup pine nuts, toasted

1½ teaspoons salt

½ cup grated Parmesan cheese

Prepare the pretzel dough as directed in the recipe.

Place the dough in a bowl sprayed with nonstick cooking spray, cover with plastic wrap, and let it rest overnight in the refrigerator.

To make the filling, place the basil leaves in the bowl of a food processor and pulse as you add the olive oil through the feed chute. Add the garlic, pine nuts, and salt. Process until smooth. Pour the mixture into a large bowl and stir in the Parmesan cheese. Set aside.

Punch the dough down, turn it out onto a lightly floured work surface, and cut it into 6 pieces. Use your hands to roll the dough into ropes that are about 24 inches long and 2 inches thick. With a rolling pin or buttered hands, flatten the ropes to a 2-inch width.

Spoon the pesto into a piping bag with a wide tip (or a ziplock with a corner cut off) and pipe along the center of each dough rope, leaving a ¼ inch border on all sides. Fold the dough over the filling and press it together, forming a seal. Follow the directions on pages 18-19 to shape the pretzels.

Place the pretzels on a parchment-lined baking sheet, cover them with plastic wrap, and let them rise at room temperature for 45 minutes, or until they have doubled in size.

Preheat the oven to 400°F.

Combine the baking soda and hot water in a bowl. Dip the risen pretzels in the baking soda bath, then return them to the baking sheet and brush them with egg. Sprinkle with the desired toppings.

Bake the pretzels for 12 minutes, or until they are golden brown. Let them cool on the baking sheet for 5 to 10 minutes before eating.

VARIATION: For chicken pesto, add 1 cup cooked diced chicken to the pesto.

Ham and Cheese Pretzels

PRETZELS

1 batch Basic Pretzel dough
(page 23)

2 teaspoons baking soda

1 cup hot water

1 egg, lightly beaten

Toppings (page 24)

FILLING

¾ cups diced ham

¾ cup shredded cheese,
your choice

2 tablespoons Dijon or
honey mustard

Prepare the pretzel dough as directed in the recipe.

Place the dough in a bowl sprayed with nonstick cooking spray, cover with plastic wrap, and let it rest overnight in the refrigerator.

To make the filling, combine the ham, cheese, and mustard in a bowl. The mixture should be slightly moist, not gooey or runny.

Punch the dough down, then turn it out onto a lightly floured work surface and cut it into 6 pieces. Use your hands to roll the dough into ropes that are about 24 inches long and 2 inches thick. With a rolling pin or buttered hands, flatten the ropes to a 2-inch width. Carefully spoon the filling into the center of each flattened rope, leaving a ¼-inch border on all sides. Fold the dough over the filling and press it together, forming a seal. Follow the directions on pages 18-19 to shape the pretzels.

Place the pretzels on a parchment-lined baking sheet, cover them with plastic wrap, and let them rise at room temperature for 45 minutes, or until they have doubled in size.

Preheat the oven to 400°F.

Combine the baking soda and hot water in a bowl. Dip the risen pretzels in the baking soda bath, then return them to the baking sheet and brush them with egg. Sprinkle with the desired toppings.

Bake the pretzels for 10 minutes, or until they are golden brown. Let them cool on the baking sheet for 5 to 10 minutes before eating.

Pepperoni and Cheese Pretzels

PRETZELS

1 batch Basic Pretzel dough
(page 23)

2 teaspoons dried rosemary

1 teaspoon dried oregano

1 teaspoon dried basil

1 teaspoon dried parsley

1 cup sun-dried tomatoes
packed in oil, drained and
minced

2 teaspoons baking soda

1 cup hot water

1 egg, lightly beaten

¼ cup grated Parmesan cheese

¼ cup shredded mozzarella
cheese

FILLING

1 cup minced pepperoni

1 cup shredded mozzarella
cheese

Prepare the pretzel dough as directed in the recipe, adding the herbs and tomatoes as you mix the proofed yeast with the flour.

Place the dough in a bowl sprayed with nonstick cooking spray, cover with plastic wrap, and let it rest overnight in the refrigerator.

Punch the dough down, then turn it out onto a lightly floured work surface and cut it into 6 pieces. Use your hands to roll the dough into ropes that are about 24 inches long and 2 inches thick. With a rolling pin or buttered hands, flatten the ropes to a 2-inch width. Carefully place the pepperoni and mozzarella cheese along the center of each flattened rope, leaving a ¼-inch border on all sides. Fold the dough over the filling and press it together, forming a seal. Follow the directions on pages 18–19 to shape the pretzels.

Place the pretzels on a parchment-lined baking sheet, cover them with plastic wrap, and let them rise at room temperature for 45 minutes, or until they have doubled in size.

Preheat the oven to 450°F.

Combine the baking soda and hot water in a bowl. Dip the risen pretzels in the baking soda bath, then return them to the baking sheet and brush them with egg.

Bake the pretzels for 15 minutes, or until they are golden brown. Let them cool on the baking sheet for 5 to 10 minutes before eating.

Remove the pretzels from the oven and sprinkle the Parmesan and mozzarella cheese onto the pretzels. Bake for another 5 minutes, or until the cheese melts and bubbles.

Pancetta, Spinach, and Ricotta Pretzels

PRETZELS

1 batch Basic Pretzel dough
  (page 23)

2 teaspoons dried rosemary

1 teaspoon dried oregano

1 teaspoon dried basil

1 teaspoon dried parsley

2 teaspoons baking soda

1 cup hot water

1 egg, lightly beaten

Toppings (page 24)

FILLING

¼ cup ricotta cheese

3 tablespoons olive oil

¼ cup minced onion

1 garlic clove, minced

4 ounces pancetta, cubed

1 cup baby spinach

¼ teaspoon pepper

⅛ teaspoon ground nutmeg

⅛ teaspoon red pepper flakes

1½ tablespoons Parmesan
  cheese

Prepare the pretzel dough as directed in the recipe, adding the herbs as you mix the proofed yeast with the flour.

Place the dough in a bowl sprayed with nonstick cooking spray, cover with plastic wrap, and let it rest overnight in the refrigerator.

To make the filling, place the ricotta cheese in a strainer lined with cheesecloth or a coffee filter and drain it of excess liquid. (The cheese should have very little moisture, to keep the filling from making the pretzels soggy.) Refrigerate in the strainer for at least 1 hour.

Heat the olive oil in a large skillet over medium heat. Add the onions, garlic, and pancetta. Sauté for 7 minutes, or until the onions are translucent and the pancetta is slightly crispy. Add the spinach and toss for 4 minutes, or until the spinach is heated through. Add the pepper, nutmeg, and red pepper flakes and stir until incorporated. Set aside to cool. Drain any excess moisture from the cool mixture.

When the ricotta has drained, add it to the spinach mixture, along with the Parmesan cheese, and stir to combine.

Punch the dough down, then turn it out onto a lightly floured work surface and cut it into 6 pieces. Use your hands to roll the dough into ropes that are about 24 inches long and 2 inches thick. With a rolling pin or buttered hands, flatten the ropes to a 2-inch width. Carefully spoon the filling along the center of each flattened rope, leaving a ¼-inch border on all sides. Fold the dough over the filling and press it together, forming a seal. Follow the directions on pages 18–19 to shape the pretzels.

Place the pretzels on a parchment-lined baking sheet, cover them with plastic wrap, and let them rise at room temperature for 45 minutes, or until they have doubled in size.

continued

Preheat the oven to 400°F.

Combine the baking soda and hot water in a bowl. Dip the risen pretzels in the baking soda bath, then return them to the baking sheet and brush them with egg.

Bake the pretzels for 15 minutes, or until they are golden brown. Let them cool on the baking sheet for 5 to 10 minutes before eating.

Vegetable and Goat Cheese Pretzels

PRETZELS

1 batch Basic Pretzel dough
(page 23)

2 teaspoons dried rosemary

1 teaspoon dried oregano

1 teaspoon dried basil

1 teaspoon dried parsley

2 teaspoons baking soda

1 cup hot water

1 egg, lightly beaten

Toppings (page 24)

FILLING

4 tablespoons extra-virgin
olive oil

2 garlic cloves, minced

½ cup diced red onion

1 green bell pepper, diced

1 red bell pepper, diced

1 small zucchini, diced

½ cup minced mushrooms

1 teaspoon kosher salt

1 teaspoon pepper

6 ounces herbed goat cheese

Prepare the pretzel dough as directed in the recipe, adding the herbs as you mix the proofed yeast with the flour.

Place the dough in a bowl sprayed with nonstick cooking spray, cover with plastic wrap, and let it rest overnight in the refrigerator.

To make the filling, heat the olive oil in a large skillet over medium heat. Add the garlic, onion, and peppers. Cook for 6 minutes, until the vegetables soften, then add the zucchini, mushrooms, salt, and pepper. Cook for 4 to 5 minutes, or until the liquid that comes from the mushrooms cooks away. Set aside to cool.

Add the goat cheese and stir to combine.

Punch the dough down, then turn it out onto a lightly floured work surface and cut it into 6 pieces. Use your hands to roll the dough into ropes that are about 24 inches long and 2 inches thick. With a rolling pin or buttered hands, flatten the ropes to a 2-inch width. Carefully spoon the filling along the center of each flattened rope, leaving a ¼-inch border on all sides. Fold the dough over the filling and press it together, forming a seal. Follow the directions on pages 18–19 to shape the pretzels.

Place the pretzels on a parchment-lined baking sheet, cover them with plastic wrap, and let them rise at room temperature for 45 minutes, or until they have doubled in size.

Preheat the oven to 400°F.

Combine the baking soda and hot water in a bowl. Dip the risen pretzels in the baking soda bath, then return them to the baking sheet and brush them with egg. Sprinkle with the desired toppings.

Bake the pretzels for 12 minutes, or until they are golden brown. Let them cool on the baking sheet for 5 to 10 minutes before eating.

Mushroom Pretzels

PRETZELS

1 batch Basic Pretzel dough (page 23)

2 teaspoons dried rosemary

1 teaspoon dried oregano

1 teaspoon dried basil

1 teaspoon dried parsley

2 teaspoons baking soda

1 cup hot water

1 egg, lightly beaten

Toppings (page 24)

FILLING

3 tablespoons unsalted butter

1 garlic clove, minced

1 small shallot, diced

1 medium leek, white parts only, diced

¾ cup minced mushrooms, such as button, Portabella, or crimini

2 tablespoons extra-dry vermouth

Salt and pepper

Prepare the pretzel dough as directed in the recipe, adding the herbs as you mix the proofed yeast with the flour.

Place the dough in a bowl sprayed with nonstick cooking spray, cover with plastic wrap, and let it rest overnight in the refrigerator.

To make the filling, melt the butter in a large sauté pan over medium heat. Add the garlic, shallot, and leek. Sauté for 6 minutes, until the vegetables are soft. Add the mushrooms and cook, stirring constantly, until they release their liquid, about 5 minutes.

Increase the heat to medium-high and add the vermouth. Cook for 5 minutes, until the liquid has completely evaporated. Remove from the heat and season to taste with salt and pepper. Set aside to cool.

Punch the dough down, then turn it out onto a lightly floured work surface and cut it into 6 pieces. Use your hands to roll the dough into ropes that are about 24 inches long and 2 inches thick. With a rolling pin or buttered hands, flatten the ropes to a 2-inch width. Carefully spoon the filling along the center of each flattened rope, leaving a ¼-inch border on all sides. Fold the dough over the filling and press it together, forming a seal. Follow the directions on pages 18–19 to shape the pretzels.

Place the pretzels on a parchment-lined baking sheet, cover them with plastic wrap, and let them rise at room temperature for 45 minutes, or until they have doubled in size.

Preheat the oven to 400°F.

Combine the baking soda and hot water in a bowl. Dip the risen pretzels in the baking soda bath, then return them to the baking sheet and brush them with egg. Sprinkle with the desired toppings.

Bake the pretzels for 15 minutes, or until they are golden brown. Let them cool on the baking sheet for 5 to 10 minutes before eating.

Tapenade Pretzels

PRETZELS

1 batch Basic Pretzel dough (page 23)

2 teaspoons dried rosemary

1 teaspoon dried oregano

1 teaspoon dried basil

1 teaspoon dried parsley

2 teaspoons baking soda

1 cup hot water

1 egg, lightly beaten

Toppings (page 24)

FILLING

40 Kalamata olives, pitted

2 tablespoons capers, rinsed and drained

2 teaspoons lemon juice

1 teaspoon anchovy paste

4 teaspoons extra-virgin olive oil

Freshly ground pepper

Prepare the pretzel dough as directed in the recipe, adding the herbs as you mix the proofed yeast with the flour.

Place the dough in a bowl sprayed with nonstick cooking spray, cover with plastic wrap, and let it rest overnight in the refrigerator.

To make the filling, place the olives, capers, lemon juice, and anchovy paste in the bowl of a food processor and pulse for 20 seconds. Drizzle the olive oil in slowly as you pulse, processing until a smooth paste forms. Season with pepper to taste and set aside.

Punch the dough down, then turn it out onto a lightly floured work surface and cut it into 6 pieces. Use your hands to roll the dough into ropes that are about 24 inches long and 2 inches thick. With a rolling pin or buttered hands, flatten the ropes to a 2-inch width.

Spoon the filling into a piping bag with a wide tip (or a ziplock with a corner cut off) and pipe along the center of each dough rope, leaving a ¼-inch border on all sides. Fold the dough over the filling and press it together, forming a seal. Follow the directions on pages 18–19 to shape the pretzels.

Place the pretzels on a parchment-lined baking sheet, cover them with plastic wrap, and let them rise at room temperature for 45 minutes, or until they have doubled in size.

Preheat the oven to 400°F.

Combine the baking soda and hot water in a bowl. Dip the risen pretzels in the baking soda bath, then return them to the baking sheet and brush them with egg. Sprinkle with the desired toppings.

Bake the pretzels for 15 minutes, or until they are golden brown. Let them cool on the baking sheet for 5 to 10 minutes before eating.

Pretzel Egg Rolls

PRETZELS

1 batch Basic Pretzel dough (page 23)

2 teaspoons baking soda

1 cup hot water

Toppings (page 24)

FILLING

3 tablespoons vegetable oil

2 garlic cloves, minced

1 tablespoon grated ginger

¼ pound ground pork

¼ cup soy sauce

⅓ cup Hoisin Pretzel Dip (page 167)

1 cup finely shredded cabbage

½ cup bean sprouts

1 small celery stalk, thinly sliced

Prepare the pretzel dough as directed in the recipe.

Place the dough in a bowl sprayed with nonstick cooking spray, cover with plastic wrap, and let it rest overnight in the refrigerator.

To make the filling, heat the oil in a skillet over medium heat. Add the garlic and ginger and cook for 2 minutes, then add the pork. Add half the soy sauce and stir, breaking up large chunks of meat. Cook until the meat is cooked but not browned crisp, about 7 minutes. Remove from the heat and add half the hoisin sauce. Set aside to cool.

Place the cabbage, bean sprouts, and celery in a bowl with the remaining soy sauce and stir well. When the meat mixture has cooled completely, combine with the vegetables.

Punch the dough down, then turn it out onto a lightly floured work surface and cut it into 6 pieces. Use your hands to roll the dough into ropes that are about 24 inches long and 2 inches thick. With a rolling pin or buttered hands, flatten the ropes to a 2-inch width. Carefully spoon the filling along the center of each flattened rope, leaving a ¼-inch border on all sides. Fold the dough over the filling and press it together, forming a seal. Follow the directions on pages 18-19 to shape the pretzels.

Place the pretzels on a parchment-lined baking sheet, cover them with plastic wrap, and let them rise at room temperature for 45 minutes, or until they have doubled in size.

Preheat the oven to 400°F.

Combine the baking soda and hot water in a bowl. Dip the risen pretzels in the baking soda bath, then return them to the baking sheet and brush them with the remaining hoisin sauce. Sprinkle with the desired toppings.

Bake the pretzels for 15 minutes, or until they are golden brown. Let them cool on the baking sheet for 5 to 10 minutes before eating.

Tomato-Hummus Pretzels

PRETZELS

1 batch Basic Pretzel dough (page 23)

2 teaspoons dried rosemary

1 teaspoon dried oregano

1 teaspoon dried basil

1 teaspoon dried parsley

1 cup sun-dried tomatoes packed in oil, drained and minced, optional

2 teaspoons baking soda

1 cup hot water

1 egg, lightly beaten

Toppings (page 24)

FILLING

1 cup hummus

Prepare the pretzel dough as directed in the recipe, adding the herbs and tomatoes as you mix the proofed yeast with the flour.

Place the dough in a bowl sprayed with nonstick cooking spray, cover with plastic wrap, and let it rest overnight in the refrigerator.

Punch the dough down, then turn it out onto a lightly floured work surface and cut it into 6 pieces. Use your hands to roll the dough into ropes that are about 24 inches long and 2 inches thick. With a rolling pin or buttered hands, flatten the ropes to a 2-inch width.

Spoon the hummus into a piping bag with a wide tip (or a ziplock with a corner cut off) and pipe along the center of each dough rope, leaving a ¼-inch border on all sides. Fold the dough over the filling and press it together, forming a seal. Follow the directions on pages 18-19 to shape the pretzels.

Place the pretzels on a parchment-lined baking sheet, cover them with plastic wrap, and let them rise at room temperature for 45 minutes, or until they have doubled in size.

Preheat the oven to 400°F.

Combine the baking soda and hot water in a bowl. Dip the risen pretzels in the baking soda bath, then return them to the baking sheet and brush them with egg. Sprinkle with the desired toppings.

Bake the pretzels for 10 minutes, or until they are golden brown. Let them cool on the baking sheet for 5 to 10 minutes before eating.

Sausage and Cheese Pretzels

PRETZELS

1 batch Basic Pretzel dough
  (page 23)

2 teaspoons dried rosemary

1 teaspoon dried oregano

1 teaspoon dried basil

1 teaspoon dried parsley

1 cup sun-dried tomatoes
  packed in oil, drained and
  minced, optional

2 teaspoons baking soda

1 cup hot water

1 egg, lightly beaten

Toppings (page 24)

FILLING

1 link sweet Italian sausage,
  casing removed and crumbled

1 link hot Italian sausage, casing
  removed and crumbled

1 shallot, diced

¼ cup red wine

¾ cups shredded mozzarella
  cheese

Prepare the pretzel dough as directed in the recipe, adding the herbs and tomatoes as you mix the proofed yeast with the flour.

Place the dough in a bowl sprayed with nonstick cooking spray, cover with plastic wrap, and let it rest overnight in the refrigerator.

To make the filling, sauté the sausages and shallot in a large skillet over medium heat, for 5 minutes, until the sausages begin to brown. Add the wine, lower the heat to medium-low, and cover. Cook for 5 minutes, or until the sausage is cooked through. Uncover the skillet and set aside to cool.

Punch the dough down, then turn it out onto a lightly floured work surface and cut it into 6 pieces. Use your hands to roll the dough into ropes that are about 24 inches long and 2 inches thick. With a rolling pin or buttered hands, flatten the ropes to a 2-inch width. Carefully spoon the filling along the center of each flattened rope, leaving a ¼-inch border on all sides. Top the filling with sprinkles of mozzarella cheese. Fold the dough over the filling and press it together, forming a seal. Follow the directions on pages 18–19 to shape the pretzels.

Place the pretzels on a parchment-lined baking sheet, cover them with plastic wrap, and let them rise at room temperature for 45 minutes, or until they have doubled in size.

Preheat the oven to 400°F.

Combine the baking soda and hot water in a bowl. Dip the risen pretzels in the baking soda bath, then return them to the baking sheet and brush them with egg. Sprinkle with the desired toppings.

Bake the pretzels for 10 minutes, or until they are golden brown. Let them cool on the baking sheet for 5 to 10 minutes before eating.

Meatball and Cheese Pretzels—"The Pretzone"

PRETZELS

1 batch Basic Pretzel dough
  (page 23)

2 teaspoons dried rosemary

1 teaspoon dried oregano

1 teaspoon dried basil

1 teaspoon dried parsley

1 cup sun-dried tomatoes,
  minced

2 teaspoons baking soda

1 cup hot water

1 egg, lightly beaten

MEATBALLS

⅛ pound ground beef

⅛ pound ground veal

⅛ pound ground pork

¼ cup Italian style breadcrumbs

2 tablespoons grated
  Parmesan cheese

1 egg

6 ounces garlic and herb
  tomato paste

1½ cups shredded mozzarella
  cheese

Prepare the pretzel dough as directed in the recipe, adding the herbs and tomatoes as you mix the proofed yeast with the flour.

Place the dough in a bowl sprayed with nonstick cooking spray, cover with plastic wrap, and let it rest overnight in the refrigerator.

Preheat the oven to 375°F.

To make the meatballs, combine the meats, breadcrumbs, Parmesan cheese, and egg in a bowl and mix with your hands until all ingredients are incorporated. Using a melon baller or a teaspoon, form very small meatballs and place them on a parchment-lined baking sheet. Bake the meatballs for 12 minutes, or until they brown.

Combine the tomato paste and ¾ cup water in a saucepan over low heat. Stir to combine. If the sauce is too thick, add more water. Add the meatballs and cook for 10 minutes. Set aside to cool.

Punch the dough down, turn it out onto a lightly floured work surface, and cut it into 6 pieces. Use your hands to roll the dough into ropes that are about 24 inches long and 2 inches thick. With a rolling pin or buttered hands, flatten the ropes to a 2-inch width. Carefully spoon the filling along the center of each flattened rope, leaving a ¼-inch border on all sides. Sprinkle the filling with mozzarella cheese. Fold the dough over the filling and press it together, forming a seal. Follow the directions on pages 18-19 to shape the pretzels.

Place the pretzels on a parchment-lined baking sheet, cover them with plastic wrap, and let them rise at room temperature for 45 minutes, or until they have doubled in size.

Preheat the oven to 400°F.

Combine the baking soda and hot water in a bowl. Dip the risen

continued

pretzels in the baking soda bath, then return them to the baking sheet and brush them with egg.

Bake the pretzels for 12 minutes, or until they are golden brown. Let them cool on the baking sheet for 5 to 10 minutes before eating.

Meatball Pretzel Bites

PRETZELS

1 batch Basic Pretzel dough (page 23)

2 teaspoons dried rosemary

1 teaspoon dried oregano

1 teaspoon dried basil

1 teaspoon dried parsley

1 cup sun-dried tomatoes packed in oil, drained and minced

2 teaspoons baking soda

1 cup hot water

1 egg, lightly beaten

MEATBALLS

⅛ pound ground beef

⅛ pound ground veal

⅛ pound ground pork

¼ cup Italian style breadcrumbs

2 tablespoons grated Parmesan cheese

Prepare the pretzel dough as directed in the recipe, adding the herbs and tomatoes as you mix the proofed yeast with the flour.

Place the dough in a bowl sprayed with nonstick cooking spray, cover with plastic wrap, and let it rest overnight in the refrigerator.

Preheat the oven to 375°F.

To make the meatballs, combine the meats, breadcrumbs, Parmesan cheese, and egg in a bowl and mix with your hands until all ingredients are incorporated. Using a melon baller or a teaspoon, form small meatballs and place them on a parchment-lined baking sheet. Bake the meatballs for 12 minutes, or until they brown.

Combine the tomato paste and ¾ cup water in a saucepan over low heat. Stir to combine. If the sauce is too thick, add more water. Add the meatballs and cook for 10 minutes. Set aside to cool.

Punch the dough down, turn it out onto a lightly floured work surface, and cut it into 48 pieces. Use your hands to roll each piece into a ball, place the balls on a parchment-lined baking sheet, cover them with plastic wrap, and let them rise at room temperature for 45 minutes, or until they have doubled in size.

Preheat the oven to 375°F.

Combine the baking soda and hot water in a bowl. Dip the risen pretzel balls in the baking soda bath, then return them to the baking sheet and brush them with egg.

1 egg

6 ounces garlic and herb
tomato paste

FILLING

¼ cup sun-dried tomatoes
packed in oil, drained and
minced

24 basil leaves

¼ cup shredded mozzarella
cheese

Flatten each ball slightly, then top 24 of them with a teaspoon of sun-dried tomatoes, a basil leaf, and a meatball. Sprinkle with mozzarella cheese and top with another ball of dough. Press to seal the dough, completely enclosing the filling.

Bake the pretzel balls for 20 minutes, or until they are golden brown. Let them cool on the baking sheet for 5 to 10 minutes before eating.

Sausage and Apple Pretzels

PRETZELS

1 batch Basic Pretzel dough
(page 23)

2 teaspoons baking soda

1 cup hot water

1 egg, lightly beaten

Toppings (page 24)

FILLING

½ pound sage or breakfast
sausage

1 cup disced onion

1 Granny Smith apple, peeled,
cored, and diced

Prepare the pretzel dough as directed in the recipe.

Place the dough in a bowl sprayed with nonstick cooking spray, cover with plastic wrap, and let it rest overnight in the refrigerator.

To make the filling, sauté the sausage and onion in a skillet over medium-high heat. Cook for 7 minutes, or until the onion is soft and the sausage is cooked. Add the apple and toss. Remove from the heat and drain off any excess grease.

Punch the dough down, then turn it out onto a lightly floured work surface and cut it into 6 pieces. Use your hands to roll the dough into ropes that are about 24 inches long and 2 inches thick. With a rolling pin or buttered hands, flatten the ropes to a 2-inch width. Carefully spoon the filling along the center of each flattened rope, leaving a ¼-inch border on all sides. Fold the dough over the filling and press it together, forming a seal. Follow the directions on pages 18–19 to shape the pretzels.

Place the pretzels on a parchment-lined baking sheet, cover them with plastic wrap, and let them rise at room temperature for 45 minutes, or until they have doubled in size.

Preheat the oven to 400°F.

Combine the baking soda and hot water in a bowl. Dip the risen pretzels in the baking soda bath, then return them to the baking sheet and brush them with egg. Sprinkle with the desired toppings.

Bake the pretzels for 10 minutes, or until they are golden brown. Let them cool on the baking sheet for 5 to 10 minutes before eating.

Aussie Meat Pie Pretzels

PRETZELS

1 batch Basic Pretzel dough
(page 23)

2 teaspoons baking soda

1 cup hot water

1 egg, lightly beaten

Toppings (page 24)

FILLING

½ pound ground beef

½ cup beef stock

1 cup minced onion

2 tablespoons all-purpose flour

1 teaspoon Worcestershire
sauce

Salt and pepper

Prepare the pretzel dough as directed in the recipe.

Place the dough in a bowl sprayed with nonstick cooking spray, cover with plastic wrap, and let it rest overnight in the refrigerator.

To make the filling, combine the beef, stock, onion, flour, Worcestershire sauce, and salt and pepper to taste in a heavy saucepan over medium-high heat. Cook for 10 minutes, stirring. Bring to a boil, then reduce the heat to low. Cover and cook for 30 to 40 minutes, stirring occasionally, or until the meat is cooked through. Set aside to cool.

Punch the dough down, then turn it out onto a lightly floured work surface and cut it into 6 pieces. Use your hands to roll the dough into ropes that are about 24 inches long and 2 inches thick. With a rolling pin or buttered hands, flatten the ropes to a 2-inch width. Carefully spoon the filling along the center of each flattened rope, leaving a ¼-inch border on all sides. Fold the dough over the filling and press it together, forming a seal. Follow the directions on pages 18–19 to shape the pretzels.

Place the pretzels on a parchment-lined baking sheet, cover them with plastic wrap, and let them rise at room temperature for 45 minutes, or until they have doubled in size.

Preheat the oven to 400°F.

Combine the baking soda and hot water in a bowl. Dip the risen pretzels in the baking soda bath, then return them to the baking sheet and brush them with egg. Sprinkle with the desired toppings.

Bake the pretzels for 10 minutes, or until they are golden brown. Let them cool on the baking sheet for 5 to 10 minutes before eating.

Chicken Cordon Bleu Pretzels

PRETZELS

1 batch Basic Pretzel dough
   (page 23)

2 teaspoons baking soda

1 cup hot water

1 egg, lightly beaten

Toppings (page 24)

FILLING

1 chicken breast, poached
   and diced

4 ounces Swiss cheese, diced

4 ounces cooked ham, diced

¼ cup Dijon mustard

Prepare the pretzel dough as directed in the recipe.

Place the dough in a bowl sprayed with nonstick cooking spray, cover with plastic wrap, and let it rest overnight in the refrigerator.

Combine the chicken, cheese, ham, and mustard in a bowl.

Punch the dough down, then turn it out onto a lightly floured work surface and cut it into 6 pieces. Use your hands to roll the dough into ropes that are about 24 inches long and 2 inches thick. With a rolling pin or buttered hands, flatten the ropes to a 2-inch width. Carefully spoon the filling along the center of each flattened rope, leaving a ¼-inch border on all sides. Fold the dough over the filling and press it together, forming a seal. Follow the directions on pages 18–19 to shape the pretzels.

Place the pretzels on a parchment-lined baking sheet, cover them with plastic wrap, and let them rise at room temperature for 45 minutes, or until they have doubled in size.

Preheat the oven to 400°F.

Combine the baking soda and hot water in a bowl. Dip the risen pretzels in the baking soda bath, then return them to the baking sheet and brush them with egg. Sprinkle with the desired toppings.

Bake the pretzels for 10 minutes, or until they are golden brown. Let them cool on the baking sheet for 5 to 10 minutes before eating.

MOVE OVER DIRTY WATER HOT DOG!

Amazingly enough, street vendors started selling their pretzels around the year 1483. They had to push portable ovens around to keep them warm!

Barbecued Chicken Pretzels

PRETZELS

1 batch Basic Pretzel dough
(page 23)

2 teaspoons baking soda

1 cup hot water

¼ cup barbecue sauce

Toppings (page 24)

FILLING

¼ cup barbecue sauce

1 cup shredded or diced
cooked barbecue chicken

Prepare the pretzel dough as directed in the recipe.

Place the dough in a bowl sprayed with nonstick cooking spray, cover with plastic wrap, and let it rest overnight in the refrigerator.

Punch the dough down, turn it out onto a lightly floured work surface, and cut it into 6 pieces. Use your hands to roll the dough into ropes that are about 24 inches long and 2 inches thick. With a rolling pin or buttered hands, flatten the ropes to a 2-inch width.

Combine the barbecue sauce and the chicken. Carefully spoon the filling along the center of each flattened rope, leaving a ¼-inch border on all sides. Fold the dough over the filling and press it together, forming a seal. Follow the directions on pages 18–19 to shape the pretzels.

Place the pretzels on a parchment-lined baking sheet, cover them with plastic wrap, and let them rise at room temperature for 45 minutes, or until they have doubled in size.

Preheat the oven to 400°F.

Combine the baking soda and hot water in a bowl. Dip the risen pretzels in the baking soda bath, then return them to the baking sheet and brush them with the barbecue sauce. Sprinkle with the desired toppings.

Bake the pretzels for 15 minutes, or until the barbecue sauce is dark brown. Let cool on the baking sheet for 5 to 10 minutes before eating.

PRETZELWICHES

Breakfast Pretzelwich

MAKES 6 SERVINGS

6 Basic Pretzels (page 23)

4 tablespoons butter

1 cup diced yellow onion

1 cup diced green bell pepper

12 eggs, beaten

½ cup minced cooked ham, bacon, or sausage

Prepare and bake the pretzels according to the recipe. Set them aside to cool.

In a large skillet set over medium heat, melt the butter, then add the onion and green bell pepper. Cook for 5 minutes, or until the vegetables soften. Add the eggs and scramble for about 5 minutes—the eggs will still be slightly uncooked. Stir in the meat and cook for about a minute or two longer until the eggs are almost done to your taste. Remove from the heat. The residual heat will continue to cook the eggs.

Slice the pretzels in half horizontally. Top each pretzel bottom with scrambled eggs then the top half of the pretzel.

VARIATIONS: You can also add salsa, diced jalapeños, or your favorite cheese to these eggs. Or top them with slices of avocado.

Lox and Cream Cheese Pretzelwich

MAKES 6 SERVINGS

6 Basic Pretzels (page 23)

8 ounces cream cheese,
  softened

8 ounces smoked salmon

1 small tomato, sliced

1 small red onion, sliced

Prepare and bake the pretzels according to the recipe. Set them aside to cool.

Slice the pretzels in half horizontally. Spread cream cheese over each bottom half, then top with salmon, tomato, onion, and the top half of the pretzel.

Salad Pretzelwich

MAKES 6 SERVINGS

6 Basic Pretzels (page 23)

1 head romaine lettuce,
  shredded

1 head Boston lettuce,
  shredded

1 large red onion, sliced

2 tomatoes, sliced

1 cucumber, peeled and sliced

1 cup grated cheese of
  your choice

2 cups salad dressing of
  your choice

Prepare and bake the pretzels according to the recipe. Set them aside to cool.

Combine the lettuces, onion, tomatoes, cucumber, cheese, and dressing in a large bowl and stir to combine thoroughly.

Slice the pretzels in half horizontally. Top each bottom half with salad then the top half of the pretzel.

Egg Salad Pretzelwich

MAKES 6 SERVINGS

6 Basic Pretzels (page 23)

6 hard-boiled eggs, mashed

1 celery stalk, minced

3 tablespoons minced onion

2 tablespoons pickle relish

1 cup mayonnaise

Prepare and bake the pretzels according to the recipe. Set them aside to cool.

Combine the eggs, celery, onion, relish, and mayonnaise in a bowl and stir to combine thoroughly.

Slice the pretzels in half horizontally. Top each bottom half with egg salad then the top half of the pretzel.

A TWIST ON THE EASTER EGG

Beginning in the mid-1500s, Germans began an Easter tradition of eating pretzels and hard-boiled eggs for Good Friday dinner. The pretzels symbolized everlasting life, while the eggs, nestled in each of the three puffy pretzel curves, represented the renewal of life.

BLTP—Bacon, Lettuce, and Tomato Pretzelwich

MAKES 6 SERVINGS

6 Basic Pretzels (page 23)

¼ cup mayonnaise

12 slices cooked bacon

6 leaves romaine lettuce

1 small tomato, sliced

Prepare and bake the pretzels according to the recipe. Set them aside to cool.

Slice the pretzels in half horizontally. Spread mayonnaise over each half, or as desired. Top each bottom half with bacon, lettuce, tomato, and the top half of the pretzel.

Cheese, Tomato, and Black Forest Ham Pretzelwich

MAKES 6 SERVINGS

6 Basic Pretzels (page 23)

6 tablespoons mayonnaise

6 tablespoons Dijon mustard

12 slices Black Forest ham

12 slices deli cheese of your choice

1 tomato, sliced

Prepare and bake the pretzels according to the recipe. Set them aside to cool.

Slice the pretzels in half horizontally and spread the tops and bottoms with mayonnaise and mustard. Top each bottom half with ham, cheese, tomato, and the top half of the pretzel.

VARIATION: You can also make these pretzelwiches with the Jalapeño Pepper and Jack Cheese Pretzels or the Parmesan Cheese Pretzels on pages 27 and 37.

Italian Hero Pretzelwich

MAKES 6 SERVINGS

6 Basic Pretzels (page 23)

½ cup extra-virgin olive oil

¾ cup wine vinegar

½ teaspoon garlic powder

½ teaspoon dried oregano

½ teaspoon dried basil

1 head romaine lettuce,
  shredded

12 slices provolone

6 slices mortadella

6 slices salami

6 slices capocolla

6 slices good quality ham

1 (12-ounce)jar roasted red bell
  peppers, drained

1 small red onion, thinly sliced

Prepare and bake the pretzels according to the recipe. Set them aside to cool.

Whisk the olive oil, vinegar, garlic powder, oregano, and basil in a small bowl. Set aside.

Preheat the oven to 350°F.

Slice the pretzels in half horizontally. Top each bottom half with lettuce, cheese, mortadella, salami, capocolla, ham, bell pepper, and onion. Drizzle dressing on the sandwiches, then top with another slice of cheese.

Place the pretzel bottoms on a parchment-lined baking sheet and bake for 5 minutes, until the cheese melts and bubbles. Remove from the oven and top with the top half of the pretzel. Let cool for 5 to 10 minutes before eating.

Tuna Melt Pretzelwich

MAKES 6 SERVINGS

6 Basic Pretzels (page 23)

2 (6-ounce) cans solid white albacore tuna packed in water

2 celery ribs, minced

1 cup diced red onion

2 tablespoons diced bell pepper

3 tablespoons dill relish

2 radishes, diced

2 green onions, minced

5 tablespoons mayonnaise

6 slices deli cheese of your choice

Prepare and bake the pretzels according to the recipe. Set them aside to cool.

Preheat the oven to 350°F.

Meanwhile, drain the tuna and place it in a large bowl. Work the tuna with a fork or your fingers until it is smooth; there should be no large chunks when you are finished. Add the celery, onion, bell pepper, relish, radishes, green onions, and mayonnaise and stir until the mayonnaise is thoroughly incorporated.

Slice the pretzels in half horizontally. Top each bottom half with tuna salad, cheese, and the top half of the pretzel.

Place the pretzel bottoms on a parchment-lined baking sheet and bake for 5 minutes, until the cheese melts and bubbles. Remove from the oven and top with the top half of the pretzel. Let cool for 5 to 10 minutes before eating.

Reuben Pretzelwich

MAKES 6 SERVINGS

6 Basic Pretzels (page 23)

1½ cups Thousand Island dressing

2 cups sauerkraut, well drained

12 slices corned beef

6 slices Swiss cheese

Prepare and bake the pretzels according to the recipe. Set them aside to cool. Set them aside to cool.

Preheat the broiler.

Slice the pretzels in half horizontally. Spread dressing on each half. Top each bottom half with sauerkraut, corned beef, and cheese.

Place the pretzel bottoms on a parchment-lined baking sheet and broil for 3 to 5 minutes, until the cheese melts and bubbles. Remove from the oven and top with the top half of the pretzel. Let cool for 5 to 10 minutes before eating.

P-funk's Rachel Pretzelwich

MAKES 6 SERVINGS

6 Basic Pretzels (page 23)

1½ cups Thousand Island dressing

2 cups coleslaw

12 slices corned beef

6 slices Swiss cheese

Prepare and bake the pretzels according to the recipe. Set them aside to cool. Set them aside to cool.

Preheat the broiler.

Slice the pretzels in half horizontally. Spread dressing on each half. Tope each bottom half with coleslaw, corned beef, and cheese.

Place the pretzel bottoms on a parchment-lined baking sheet and broil for 3 to 5 minutes, until the cheese melts and bubbles. Remove from the oven and top with the top half of the pretzel. Let cool for 5 to 10 minutes before eating.

VARIATION: You can also make both of the pretzelwiches on this page with the Caraway Seed Pretzels on page 24.

Croque Monsieur Pretzelwich

MAKES 6 SERVINGS

6 Basic Pretzels (page 23)

2 tablespoons butter

3 tablespoons all-purpose flour

1½ cups milk

1½ cups shredded Swiss cheese

1 teaspoon kosher salt

1 teaspoon pepper

Dijon mustard

12 slices ham

6 slices Swiss cheese

Prepare and bake the pretzels according to the recipe. Set them aside to cool.

Heat the butter in a heavy saucepan over medium heat. Whisk in the flour and cook until the mixture thickens, about 5 minutes. Remove from the heat and add the milk, shredded cheese, salt, and pepper. Whisk until thoroughly combined. Set aside.

Preheat the broiler.

Slice the pretzels in half horizontally. Spread each bottom half with mustard, then top with ham, cheese, and the top half of the pretzel.

Place the sandwiches on a parchment-lined baking sheet. Pour 3 tablespoons of cheese sauce over each sandwich and broil for 1 minute, until the sauce begins to bubble and brown. Serve immediately.

A WHAT WICH?!

In Southern Germany and Switzerland, thick
soft pretzels have been sliced horizontally and used to
make sandwiches, called *Butterbrezn*, for ages!

Cheeseburger Pretzelwich

MAKES 6 SERVINGS

6 Basic Pretzels (page 23)

1½ pounds ground beef

2 teaspoons seasoning salt

1 teaspoon pepper

2 teaspoons Worcestershire sauce

1 teaspoon garlic or onion powder

6 slices cheddar or American cheese

Optional toppings: ketchup, mustard, mayonnaise, sliced red onion, relish

Prepare and bake the pretzels according to the recipe. Set them aside to cool.

In a large bowl, combine the ground beef, seasoning salt, pepper, Worcestershire sauce, and garlic powder. Mix with your hands, but don't overwork the meat. The process shouldn't take longer than 5 minutes. Shape the meat into 6 hamburger patties. Fry the patties in a large skillet over medium heat for about 5 minutes on each side, depending on the level of doneness preferred. After 2 minutes on the second side, top each patty with a slice of cheese. *Do not press on the meat as it cooks and only turn the meat once.*

Slice the pretzels in half horizontally. Top each bottom half with a patty and your choice of toppings.

Chili and Cheese Pretzelwich

MAKES 6 SERVINGS

6 Basic Pretzels (page 23)

2 tablespoons vegetable oil

1 pound ground beef

1 small yellow onion, diced

1 clove garlic, minced

1 teaspoon ground cumin

½ teaspoon dried thyme

½ teaspoon dried oregano

2 teaspoons chili powder

½ teaspoon red pepper flakes

2 teaspoons salt

1 (8-ounce) can tomato sauce

1½ cups shredded cheddar cheese

2 green onions, green parts diced

Prepare and bake the pretzels according to the recipe. Set them aside to cool.

Heat the oil in a large, heavy saucepan, over medium heat. Add the beef, onion, garlic, cumin, thyme, oregano, chili powder, and red pepper flakes. Cook, stirring constantly, for 10 minutes, or until the meat turns gray and the vegetables soften.

Drain most of the oil and grease from the pan and place the pan back on the stove. Add the tomato sauce, lower the heat, and simmer for 30 to 45 minutes.

Slice the pretzels in half horizontally. Top each bottom half with chili, cheese, green onion, and the top half of the pretzel.

A CLEVER BAKER

One pretzel story tells of an Alsatian baker who had been imprisoned for insulting a lord's wife. The lord told the baker that he'd set him free if he could make him a cake "through which I can see the sun three times." When the baker presented the lord with a pretzel, the lord let the baker go.

Chicken, Bacon, and Avocado Pretzelwich

MAKES 6 SERVINGS

6 Basic Pretzels (page 23)

¼ cup mayonnaise

1 pound cooked chicken
  breast, sliced

12 slices cooked bacon

1 avocado, sliced

1 cup shredded lettuce

Prepare and bake the pretzels according to the recipe. Set them aside to cool.

Slice the pretzels in half horizontally. Spread mayonnaise on each half, then top each bottom half with chicken, bacon, avocado, lettuce, and the top half of the pretzel.

Chicken and Guacamole Pretzelwich

MAKES 6 SERVINGS

6 Basic Pretzels (page 23)

12 leaves romaine lettuce

1½ cups guacamole

12 slices cooked bacon

3 chicken breasts, grilled

Prepare and bake the pretzels according to the recipe. Set them aside to cool.

Slice the pretzels in half horizontally. Divide the lettuce evenly among the bottom halves, then top with guacamole, bacon, chicken and the top half of the pretzel.

Curried Chicken Salad Pretzelwich

MAKES 6 SERVINGS

6 Basic Pretzels (page 23)

3 tablespoons extra-virgin olive oil

1 medium onion, diced

2½ cups chicken stock

2 boneless skinless chicken thighs, cut into bite-sized pieces

1 boneless skinless chicken breast, cut into bite-sized pieces

1 teaspoon ground coriander

1 teaspoon turmeric

1 tablespoon garam masala, optional

1 jalapeño, Scotch bonnet, or Thai chili pepper, minced, optional

¾ cup mayonnaise

1 tablespoon curry powder

Pinch of salt

½ cup finely minced celery, including leafy part

1 green onion, green parts minced

¼ cup sliced almonds, toasted

3 tablespoons raisins, plumped (see note on page 46)

Prepare and bake the pretzels according to the recipe. Set them aside to cool.

Heat the oil in a large skillet over medium heat. Add the onion and sauté for 5 minutes, until soft and translucent. Set aside to cool.

Bring the stock to a boil in a large stock pot over high heat. Add the chicken, coriander, turmeric, garam masala, and chili pepper and cook for 12 minutes, until the chicken is cooked through.

Using a slotted spoon, remove the cooked chicken from the broth, and set it aside to cool.

Combine the mayonnaise, curry powder, and pinch of salt. Refrigerate until ready to use.

In a large bowl, combine the chicken, curry mayonnaise, sautéed onions, celery, green onion, almonds, and raisins.

Slice the pretzels in half horizontally. Top each bottom half with chicken curry salad and the top half of the pretzel.

Asian Chicken Pretzelwich

MAKES 6 SERVINGS

6 Basic Pretzels (page 23)

¼ cup Hoisin Pretzel
  Dip (page 167)

1½ tablespoons cornstarch

2 boneless, skinless chicken
  breast halves, cut into bite-
  sized pieces

3 tablespoons vegetable oil

1 teaspoon sesame oil

1½ teaspoons rice wine vinegar

2 tablespoons soy sauce

2 teaspoons minced ginger

2 garlic cloves, minced

1 tablespoon brown sugar

1 yellow onion, sliced

½ cup snow peas

1 green or red bell pepper,
  sliced

½ cup sliced mushrooms

1 carrot, peeled and sliced

¼ cup chicken stock

Prepare and bake the pretzels according to the recipe. At the last 5 minutes of baking, brush them with the Hoisin Dipping Sauce, then continue baking. Set aside to cool.

Combine the cornstarch and chicken in a bowl.

Combine the vegetable oil, sesame oil, vinegar, ginger, garlic, and brown sugar in a bowl. Whisk to combine. Pour the oil mixture into a large skillet over high heat. When the oil is hot, add the chicken and stir fry for 3 to 5 minutes, until the chicken loses its pink color and is just cooked. Remove the chicken from the pan and place in a bowl.

Add additional oil to the skillet if needed, then cook the onion, peas, bell pepper, mushrooms, and carrot. Toss quickly, moving the vegetables around the pan so they don't scorch. After 5 minutes, return the chicken to the pan and add the chicken stock. Cook for 5 minutes.

Slice the pretzels in half horizontally. Top each bottom half with the stir fry.

Chicken Fajita Pretzelwich

MAKES 6 SERVINGS

6 Basic Pretzels (page 23)

1 teaspoon chili powder

1 teaspoon kosher salt

½ teaspoon ground cumin

1 teaspoon onion powder

½ teaspoon garlic powder

1 tablespoon cornstarch

¼ cup water

3 tablespoons extra-virgin
olive oil

2 boneless, skinless chicken
breast halves, cut into strips

1 green bell pepper,
cut into strips

1 medium yellow onion,
thinly sliced

¼ cup minced cilantro

2 tablespoons lime juice

Shredded cheese, guacamole,
sour cream, shredded lettuce,
to serve

Prepare and bake the pretzels according to the recipe. Set them aside to cool.

Combine the chili powder, salt, cumin, onion powder, garlic powder, cornstarch, water, and 2 tablespoons of the oil in a ziplock plastic bag. Add the chicken, pepper, and onion. Seal and knead the bag to mix the ingredients. Refrigerate for 30 minutes.

Heat the remaining 1 tablespoon oil in a large skillet over high heat. Empty the contents of the bag into the skillet and cook, stirring constantly, for 6 minutes, until the chicken is cooked thoroughly. Remove from the heat and sprinkle with cilantro and lime juice.

Slice the pretzels in half horizontally. Spoon fajitas over the bottoms of the pretzels and top with the top half of the pretzel. Serve with lettuce, cheese, sour cream, and guacamole.

Turkey and Brie Pretzelwich

MAKES 6 SERVINGS

6 Basic Pretzels (page 23)

Dijon mustard

12 slices turkey breast

1 pound Brie cheese, sliced

1 cup seedless grapes, cut in half

Prepare and bake the pretzels according to the recipe. Set them aside to cool.

Slice the pretzels in half horizontally. Spread mustard over the tops and bottoms. Top each bottom half with turkey, Brie, grapes, and the top half of the pretzel.

HOLY PRETZELS!
Catholics have been known to eat pretzels on Fridays during Lent, the 40-day period of atonement that precedes Easter. In Roman times, Christians kept a very strict fast through Lent: eating no milk, butter, cheese, eggs, cream, or meat. Instead, they made bread out of water, flour, and salt.

Thanksgiving Pretzelwich

MAKES 6 SERVINGS

1 batch Basic Pretzel dough
  (page 23)

1 cup dried cranberries,
  plumped (see note on
  page 46)

2 teaspoons baking soda

1 cup hot water

1 egg, lightly beaten

1½ cups shredded cooked
  turkey meat

½ cup cranberry sauce

1½ cups stuffing

1 cup turkey gravy, heated

Prepare the pretzel dough as directed in the recipe, adding the cranberries as you mix the proofed yeast with the flour.

Place the dough in a bowl sprayed with nonstick cooking spray, cover with plastic wrap, and let it rest overnight in the refrigerator.

Punch the dough down, then turn it out onto a lightly floured work surface and cut it into 6 pieces. Follow the directions on pages 18-19 to shape the pretzels.

Place the pretzels on a parchment-lined baking sheet, cover them with plastic wrap, and let them rise at room temperature for 45 minutes, or until they have doubled in size.

Preheat the oven to 450°F.

Combine the baking soda and hot water in a bowl. Dip the risen pretzels in the baking soda bath, then return them to the baking sheet and brush them with egg.

Bake for 15 minutes, or until they are golden brown. Let them cool on the baking sheet for 5 to 10 minutes.

Slice the pretzels in half horizontally. Top each bottom half with turkey, cranberry sauce, stuffing, gravy, and the top half of the pretzel.

Pulled Pork Pretzelwich

MAKES 6 SERVINGS

6 Basic Pretzels (page 23)

1½ tablespoons paprika

¾ tablespoon garlic powder

½ tablespoon brown sugar

½ tablespoon ground mustard

1 teaspoon cayenne pepper

1½ tablespoons kosher salt

1 (5-pound) pork shoulder
    or butt

Barbecue sauce, for serving

Prepare and bake the pretzels according to the recipe. Set them aside to cool.

Combine the paprika, garlic powder, brown sugar, mustard, cayenne pepper, and salt. Rub this spice mixture spice over the pork and let it marinate, covered, overnight in the refrigerator. (If you are in a hurry, you can marinate the meat for 1 hour, but overnight is best.)

Preheat the oven to 300°F.

Place the pork in a large baking pan and bake for 5 to 6 hours, until an instant-read thermometer stuck in the thickest part of the pork reads 170°F. Set aside to cool slightly.

When the pork is cool enough to handle, shred it with two forks, placing the shredded meat into a large bowl. Pour enough barbecue sauce over the shredded pork to moisten it and toss until it is thoroughly incorporated.

Slice the pretzels in half horizontally. Top each bottom half with shredded pork, and the top half of the pretzel. Serve with additional barbecue sauce.

Cuban-Style Pretzelwich

MAKES 6 SERVINGS

6 Basic Pretzels (page 23)

6 garlic cloves, minced

½ teaspoon ground dried oregano

1 teaspoon salt

2 tablespoons powdered adobo seasoning

5 pound pork shoulder

Yellow mustard

12 slices ham

6 slices Swiss cheese

16 dill pickle slices

Prepare and bake the pretzels according to the recipe. Set them aside to cool.

Combine the garlic, oregano, and salt, forming a chunky paste. Using a sharp knife, cut slits into the meaty side of the pork. Stuff the garlic mixture into the slits. Sprinkle with adobo and rub it in well, being sure to cover the entire roast. Place the roast in a roasting pan, cover with foil, and let it marinate in the refrigerator overnight.

Remove the roast from the refrigerator and let it come to room temperature.

Preheat the oven to 350°F.

Place the pork skin side down in a roasting pan. Bake it, uncovered, for 2 hours.

Remove the pork from the oven and carefully turn it skin side up. Bake for 2 to 4 more hours, until an instant-read thermometer stuck into the thickest part of the roast reads 170°F. The pork skin will be crispy, the meat tender, and the juices will run clear. Set aside to cool. Cut into slices.

To assemble the pretzelwiches, slice the pretzels horizontally. Spread each half with mustard. Top the bottom halves with ham, cheese, pickle, pork, and the top half of the pretzel.

Grill the sandwich for 2 to 3 minutes in a panini grill or on a skillet, weighted down with a brick wrapped in foil.

Muffuletta Pretzelwich

MAKES 6 SERVINGS

6 Basic Pretzels (page 23)

1 cup black olives

1 cup pimiento-stuffed
green olives

1 (6-ounce) jar artichoke
hearts in oil, drained with
oil reserved

½ cup mayonnaise

½ teaspoon garlic powder

12 thin slices ham

12 thin slices salami

12 thin slices deli cheese
of your choice

Prepare and bake the pretzels according to the recipe. Set them aside to cool.

Preheat the oven to 250°F.

Combine the olives and artichoke hearts in the bowl of a food processor and process to coarse chunks. Add the mayonnaise and garlic powder and process, adding some of the artichoke oil gradually, until smooth. The mixture must be of a spreadable consistency.

Slice the pretzels in half horizontally. Spread the olive mixture on each half. Top each bottom half with ham, salami, cheese, and the top half of the pretzel. Wrap the sandwiches in foil and warm in the oven for 20 minutes.

VARIATION: You can also make these pretzelwiches with the Onion Pretzels on page 26.

Gyro Pretzelwich

- -

MAKES 6 SERVINGS

6 Basic Pretzels (page 23)

1 onion, half minced, half sliced

1 pound ground lamb

½ teaspoon finely minced garlic

½ teaspoon dried marjoram

½ teaspoon dried ground
   rosemary

1 teaspoon kosher salt

¼ teaspoon pepper

1½ cups shredded lettuce

1 diced tomato

TZATSIKI

7 ounces Greek yogurt

½ cucumber, peeled, seeded,
   and minced

Pinch kosher salt

2 garlic cloves, finely minced

1 tablespoon extra-virgin
   olive oil

1 teaspoon red wine vinegar

3 mint leaves, finely minced

Prepare and bake the pretzels according to the recipe. Set them aside to cool.

Preheat the oven to 325°F.

Combine the minced onion, lamb, garlic, marjoram, rosemary, salt, and pepper in the bowl of a food processor and process to a smooth paste, periodically scraping the sides of the work bowl. Pour the lamb mixture into a loaf pan that has been sprayed with nonstick cooking spray, or shape into a meat loaf and place on a baking sheet that has been covered with foil.

Bake for 1 hour, or until an instant-read thermometer stuck into the middle reads 160°F. Drain off any excess grease and place the loaf on a cutting board to cool. Cut into slices.

To make the tzatsiki, combine all the ingredients in a bowl and mix thoroughly. Refrigerate until you're ready to use it.

Cut the pretzels in half horizontally. Top each bottom half with meat loaf, lettuce, tomato, tzatsiki, and the top half of the pretzel.

Pretzel Taco—"The Paco"

MAKES 6 SERVINGS

6 Basic Pretzels (page 23)

1 pound ground beef

½ cup water

1 (1.25-ounce) package taco seasoning mix

1½ cups shredded lettuce

1 cup shredded Monterey Jack or cheddar cheese

1 small tomato, diced

1 small red onion, diced

1 avocado, diced

1 cup salsa

Prepare and bake the pretzels according to the recipe. Set them aside to cool.

Brown the meat in a large skillet over medium-high heat, cooking for about 5 to 10 minutes. Drain the fat from the skillet, then add the water and taco seasoning mix, stirring to incorporate. Bring to a boil, then reduce the heat and simmer for 10 to 15 minutes, until the meat is cooked through.

Slice the pretzels in half horizontally. Top each bottom half with lettuce, beef, cheese, tomato, onion, avocado, salsa, and the top half of the pretzel.

USING STORE-BOUGHT PRETZELS SNACKS

Fruity-Crunchy-Sweet Granola

MAKES ABOUT 5 CUPS

2 cups nonfat vanilla yogurt

½ cup berries, your choice, fresh or thawed

1 (11-ounce) can mandarin orange segments, drained

¾ cup granola cereal

½ cup crushed pretzels

¼ cup dried cranberries

Combine all the ingredients in a large bowl and serve in individual cups.

Sweet Pretzel Mix

MAKES ABOUT 9 CUPS

2 cups salted peanuts

1 cup pecans

1 cup cashews

1 cup candy coated chocolate pieces

1 cup raisins

1 cup chopped dates

1 cup pretzel sticks or mini pretzels

¼ cup sunflower seeds

Combine all ingredients in a large bowl and enjoy.

Hot and Spicy Pretzel Mix

MAKES ABOUT 6 CUPS

2 cups small pretzels

1 cup corn squares cereal

1 cup rice squares cereal

½ cup small cheese crackers

1 cup honey-roasted cashews

2 tablespoons butter, melted

1½ teaspoons Worcestershire sauce

1 teaspoon garlic powder

½ teaspoon chili powder

½ teaspoon ground cumin

Preheat the oven to 300°F.

In a large bowl, combine the pretzels, cereals, crackers, and cashews.

In a separate bowl, combine the butter, Worcestershire sauce, garlic powder, chili powder, and cumin. Pour the spice mixture over the dry ingredients and toss to coat. Pour this mixture into a 15 x 10-inch baking pan.

Bake, stirring halfway through cooking, for 25 minutes, or until lightly toasted. Cool completely before serving.

Trail Mix

MAKES ABOUT 6 CUPS

1 cup pretzel sticks

1 cup pretzel nuggets

1½ cups banana or
plantain chips

½ cup semisweet
chocolate chips

⅓ cup raisins

1 cup peanuts

1 cup cashews

½ cup dried fruit

Combine all ingredients in a large container or bowl and enjoy. Makes about 6 cups

Pretzel Caramel Bites

MAKES ABOUT 5 CUPS

24 pretzel nuggets

1 cup chopped caramel candies

½ cup chopped walnuts

1 cup chocolate chips

Place the pretzels in a microwave-safe bowl and top with the caramel, walnuts, and chocolate chips. Microwave for 30 seconds, or until the chocolate and caramel have melted. Set aside to cool for about 5 minutes before eating.

Popcorn and Pretzel Balls

MAKES ABOUT 2 DOZEN
(2-INCH) BALLS

2 (3.5-ounce) bags microwave
  popcorn

2 cups sugar

1½ cups water

4 tablespoons butter, softened

½ cup light corn syrup

1 teaspoon vinegar

2 teaspoons vanilla extract

2 cups broken pretzel sticks

Pop the popcorn in the microwave as directed. Set aside to cool.

Combine the sugar, water, butter, corn syrup, vinegar, and vanilla in a large saucepan set over medium-low heat. Cook, stirring, until the sugar dissolves and the mixture is smooth.

Pour the popcorn and pretzels into a very large bowl or stockpot. Carefully pour the sugar mixture over the popcorn and pretzels. Stir with a sturdy wooden spoon.

With butter-greased hands, carefully form balls with the mixture—it will be hot—and place them on a parchment-lined baking pan or baking sheets to set.

Peanut Butter Pretzel Drops

MAKES ABOUT
2 DOZEN DROPS

1 cup corn syrup

¼ cup sugar

1 cup peanut butter

2 teaspoons vanilla extract

2 cups crisp rice cereal

2 cups corn flake cereal

1 cup broken pretzels

½ cup chocolate chips

Combine the corn syrup and sugar in a heavy saucepan over medium-high heat and bring to a boil. Cook for 6 minutes. Stir in the peanut butter.

Remove from the heat and stir in the vanilla, cereals, pretzels, and chocolate chips. Use an ice cream scoop to drop the mixture onto waxed paper. Refrigerate for 1 hour, until set.

Yogurt and Chocolate Covered Pretzels

MAKES ABOUT 2 CUPS

½ pound chocolate candy coating (see note below)

2 teaspoons vanilla extract

2 cups pretzel minis

½ cup Greek yogurt

½ cup chocolate chips

Place the candy coating and vanilla in a large microwave-safe bowl and microwave, uncovered, on medium power for 90 seconds. Stir, then microwave for another 90 seconds. Stir the mixture until it is smooth. Add the pretzels and yogurt and mix to coat the pretzels thoroughly.

Spoon the dipped pretzels in an even layer onto waxed paper and let them to cool for 30 minutes, until the chocolate sets.

Melt the chocolate chips in the microwave, then use a fork to drizzle the melted chocolate over the cooled pretzels. Allow to cool before breaking apart.

NOTE: Chocolate candy coating, also known as almond bark, is not really chocolate. It's a combination of vegetable fats, artificial flavors, and food coloring, and is often found in candy/ cake decorating supply stores and craft stores. It is often sold in blocks or round discs. We found some nice ones online at www.cincicakeandcandy.com.

Pretzel Haystacks

MAKES ABOUT
16 HAYSTACKS

½ cup butterscotch chips

½ cup chocolate chips

¾ cup peanut butter

1 cup chow mein noodles

1 cup pretzel sticks

Microwave the butterscotch and chocolate chips in a microwave-safe bowl on medium power for 3 to 5 minutes, until the chips are mostly melted. Carefully stir in the peanut butter, chow mein noodles, and pretzel sticks, being sure to coat the noodles and pretzels thoroughly.

Use a large spoon to spoon out the mixture and drop it onto a wax paper-lined baking sheet. Continue in the same manner with the rest of the mixture. Refrigerate for 30 minutes to set.

ALWAYS CHEW YOUR PRETZELS!

On January 13, 2002, President George W. Bush lost consciousness for a brief time while eating a pretzel and watching a football game on television. The next day, when he appeared before reporters sporting a large red bruise on his check and a busted lip, he said, "My mother always said when you're eating pretzels, chew before you swallow."

Pretzel-Crusted Caramel Apples

MAKES 6 APPLES

1 (14-ounce) package
   caramel candies

6 wooden dowels

6 apples

¾ cup crushed pretzels

Heat the caramels in a saucepan over low heat for 10 minutes, stirring constantly, until the caramels melt completely. Carefully stick the wooden dowels into the stem end of apples and dip the apples into the caramel mixture. Roll the apples in the crushed pretzels and place on waxed paper to set.

USING STORE-BOUGHT PRETZELS
SIDES AND MAIN DISHES

Chinese Chicken Pretzel Salad

SALAD

MAKES 6 TO 8 SERVINGS

3 cups cooked chicken, shredded

2 heads iceberg lettuce, shredded

5 green onions, sliced

¼ cup minced cilantro

¼ cup sliced almonds, toasted

¼ cup sesame seeds, toasted

1½ cups crushed pretzel sticks

DRESSING

¼ cup sesame oil

¼ cup canola oil

¼ cup dark soy sauce

5 tablespoons sugar

2 tablespoons rice wine vinegar

1½ tablespoons creamy peanut butter

Freshly ground pepper

In a large salad bowl, combine the chicken, lettuce, green onions, and cilantro.

In a separate bowl, combine the sesame and canola oil, soy sauce, vinegar, peanut butter, and pepper, and whisk until thoroughly mixed. Add the dressing to the salad and toss to combine. Add the almonds, sesame seeds, and pretzel crumbs and serve.

Mandarin Chicken Salad

MAKES 6 TO 8 SERVINGS

Salad

2 cups diced cooked chicken

1 head romaine lettuce, torn

1 head Boston lettuce, torn

1 medium red onion, sliced

1 pint cherry or grape tomatoes

1 (11-ounce) can mandarin orange segments, drained

½ cup crushed pretzels

Dressing

⅓ cup sesame oil

3 tablespoons orange juice

1 garlic clove, minced

¼ cup rice wine vinegar

Freshly cracked pepper

In a large salad bowl, combine the chicken, lettuces, onions, and tomatoes.

In a separate bowl, combine the oil, orange juice, garlic, vinegar, and pepper, and whisk until thoroughly combined. Toss the dressing with the chicken mixture, then add the oranges and pretzels just before serving.

Broccoli Bake

MAKES 8 TO 10 SERVINGS

1 (18-ounce) package frozen broccoli florets, thawed

1 (10.75-ounce) can cream of mushroom soup

¾ cup milk

⅔ cup French fried onions

⅓ cup crushed pretzels

½ cup shredded cheddar cheese

Combine milk with mushroom soup, whisking to remove any lumps. Mix with broccoli and half of the pretzels and onions in a 2-quart casserole dish.

Bake at 350°F for 25 minutes. Remove from oven. Top with remaining onions, cheese and pretzels. Bake additional five minutes. Serve immediately.

Green Bean Casserole

MAKES 8 TO 10 SERVINGS

¾ cup milk

1 (10.75-ounce) can cream of mushroom soup

1 (18-ounce) package frozen green beans, thawed

⅔ cup French fried onions

¾ cup crushed pretzels

Preheat the oven to 350°F.

In a 2-quart casserole dish, combine the milk and mushroom soup, and whisk out any lumps. Add the green beans and stir to coat. Stir in half the fried onions and half the pretzels.

Bake for 25 minutes, until the mixture is bubbly, then pour the remaining onions and pretzels over the top. Bake for 5 minutes. Serve immediately.

Auntie Skettie's Spoon Bread

MAKES 8 TO 10 SERVINGS

1 (14.75-ounce) can cream-style corn

1 (11-ounce) can Mexicorn

1 (8.5-ounce) package corn muffin mix

1 cup sour cream

3 tablespoons butter

1 teaspoon garlic powder

1 egg

1 cup French fried onions

¾ cup crushed pretzels

¾ cup shredded cheddar cheese

Preheat the oven to 350°F.

Combine the creamed corn, mexicorn, muffin mix, sour cream, butter, garlic powder, egg, and ½ cup of the French fried onions in a greased 2-quart baking dish.

Bake for 40 minutes, or until the mixture is hot and bubbly.

Remove the casserole from the oven and top with the pretzels, cheese, and remaining fried onions. Bake for 5 minutes, until the cheese melts and bubbles.

Strawberry Gelatin Pretzel Salad

1 (6-ounce) package strawberry gelatin

2 cups boiling water

1 (16-ounce) package frozen strawberries, thawed

2 cups crushed pretzels

¾ cup butter, melted

3 tablespoons plus 1 cup sugar

8 ounces cream cheese, softened

2 cups whipped cream or whipped topping

Fresh strawberries, for garnish

Preheat the oven to 400°F.

Combine the gelatin with the boiling water in a large bowl. Stir to dissolve the gelatin powder. Add the strawberries and refrigerate until the gelatin sets slightly, about 15 to 20 minutes. You will be pouring the gelatin into another bowl, so it doesn't need to set completely.

Combine the pretzels, butter, and 3 tablespoons of the sugar in a large mixing bowl. Press this mixture into the bottom of a 13 x 9-inch baking pan and bake for 10 minutes. Set aside to cool.

Combine the cream cheese, whipped cream, and the remaining 1 cup of sugar in a large bowl. Use an electric mixer on medium speed to cream the mixture. Spoon into the cooled crust and refrigerate for 10 minutes.

Spoon the gelatin mixture on top of the cream cheese mixture, and refrigerate for 30 minutes until the gelatin sets completely.

To serve, garnish with strawberries.

Mac and Cheese Pretzel Bake

- -

MAKES 8 TO 10 SERVINGS

6 tablespoons butter

1 onion, minced

3 tablespoons all-purpose flour

1½ cups milk

2 pounds processed cheese, cubed

2 teaspoons garlic powder

1 (16-ounce) box elbow macaroni, cooked and drained

1 cup crushed pretzels

Preheat the oven to 350°F.

In a heavy saucepan, melt 3 tablespoons of butter over low heat. Add the onion and cook for 5 minutes, until it is translucent.

Whisk in the flour and cook for 3 minutes, until the mixture is smooth. Slowly whisk in the milk and cook, whisking constantly, until the mixture thickens. Add half the cheese and the garlic powder and stir until the cheese melts and the mixture is smooth and creamy, about 6 minutes. Remove from the heat.

Combine the macaroni with the cheese sauce in a 3-quart baking dish. Top with the remaining cheese and toss.

Bake for 15 minutes.

Meanwhile, melt the remaining 3 tablespoons butter, then toss with the pretzel crumbs. Remove the casserole from oven (after 15 minutes) and sprinkle the crumb mixture on top. Bake for 5 minutes more.

Mexi-Pretzi Bake

MAKES 6 TO 8 SERVINGS

1 cup refried beans

2 cups pretzel sticks

1½ cups shredded Monterey
  Jack cheese

1 head iceberg lettuce,
  shredded

¼ cup diced tomatoes

¼ cup diced red onions

Minced jalapeño pepper,
  for garnish

Spoon the beans into a 2-quart microwave-safe casserole dish. Sprinkle half the pretzel sticks and half the cheese over the beans and heat in the microwave for 30 seconds, until the cheese starts to melt.

Layer the lettuce, tomatoes, onions, and remaining cheese over the top of the casserole and microwave for 25 seconds, until the cheese melts. Garnish with jalapeño peppers.

Onion, Sausage, and Pretzel Stuffing

MAKES 8 TO 10 SERVINGS

8 ounces sage sausage

1 green bell pepper, diced

1 onion, diced

1 celery stalk, diced

1 cup chicken stock

3 cups dry herb stuffing

1 cup dry cornbread stuffing

1 cup crushed pretzel nuggets

Crumble the sausage into a large skillet set over medium-high heat and cook for 5 minutes. As the sausage cooks and releases its juices, add the bell pepper, onion, and celery, and cook for 7 minutes, until the vegetables are soft.

Drain off any excess grease and pour the meat mixture into a large bowl. Add the chicken stock, stuffings, and crushed pretzels and stir to incorporate.

Apple, Onion, and Pretzel Stuffing

MAKES 8 TO 10 SERVINGS

1 tablespoon butter

1 small yellow onion, minced

1 Granny Smith apple, peeled, cored, and diced

¼ cup raisins, plumped (see page 46)

¼ cup coarsely chopped pecans

¾ cup crushed pretzels

¼ cup dry breadcrumbs

½ teaspoon ground sage

Pinch of nutmeg

Pinch of allspice

Melt the butter in a medium-sized sauté pan set over medium heat. Add onion and apple and cook, stirring constantly, for 5 minutes until the onions soften and become translucent.

Remove the pan from the heat and add the remaining ingredients. Stir well to incorporate.

Apple, Sausage, and Pretzel Stuffing

MAKES 8 TO 10 SERVINGS

8 ounces sage sausage

8 ounces hot and spicy breakfast sausage

1 medium onion, diced

1 celery stalk, diced

1 Granny Smith apple

1 cup chicken stock

3 cups herb stuffing

½ cup pecans, toasted

1 cup crushed pretzel nuggets

Peel, core, and dice the apple. Crumble the sausages into a large skillet set over medium-high heat and cook for 5 minutes. As the sausage cooks and releases its juices, add the onion and celery, and cook for 7 minutes, until the vegetables are soft. Add the apple and remove from the heat.

Drain off any excess grease and transfer the meat mixture to a large bowl. Add the chicken stock, stuffing, pecans, and crushed pretzels and stir well to incorporate.

Chicken Pretzel Casserole

MAKES 8 TO 10 SERVINGS

2 cups diced cooked chicken

1½ cups minced celery

⅓ cup minced onion

1 garlic clove, minced

1 teaspoon pepper

¾ cup mayonnaise

1½ cups shredded cheddar cheese

1 cup crushed pretzels

Preheat the oven to 350°F.

Combine the chicken, celery, onion, garlic, pepper, and mayonnaise in a 2-quart casserole dish. Top with the cheese and pretzels.

Bake for 25 minutes, until the cheese starts to bubble and the casserole is cooked through.

Tuna Casserole

MAKES 8 TO 10 SERVINGS

1 (16-ounce) package
elbow macaroni, cooked

1 (10.75-ounce) can cream
of mushroom soup

1 cup milk

¼ cup minced yellow onion

1 cup frozen peas

2 (6-ounce) cans tuna, drained

½ cup crushed pretzels

3 tablespoons butter, melted

1 cup shredded cheddar cheese

Preheat the oven to 350°F.

Combine the macaroni, mushroom soup, milk, onion, peas, and tuna in a 2-quart casserole dish and stir well to incorporate.

In a separate bowl, mix the pretzels with the butter and sprinkle over the top of the casserole. Sprinkle with the cheese.

Bake for 25 minutes, until the cheese starts to bubble and the casserole is cooked through.

Ranch Pretzel Chicken

MAKES 8 TO 10 SERVINGS

1 (0.4-ounce) package
ranch dressing mix

3 boneless, skinless chicken
breasts

1 egg, lightly beaten

½ cup crushed pretzels

4 tablespoons butter, melted

Preheat the oven to 350°F.

Pour the ranch dressing mix into a ziplock bag. Add the chicken and shake to coat thoroughly. Put the egg and pretzels in separate shallow dishes. Dip the chicken into the egg and then into the pretzels. Drizzle butter over the breasts and place them on a parchment-lined baking sheet.

Bake for 15 minutes, until the chicken is golden and cooked.

Ground Beef Casserole

MAKES 8 TO 10 SERVINGS

1 medium onion, minced

3 tablespoons butter

1½ pounds ground beef

8 ounces tomato sauce

4 ounces green chilies, drained

2 eggs, lightly beaten

1 cup half-and-half

Salt and pepper

1½ cups corn chips

½ cup crushed pretzels

1 cup shredded Monterey
Jack cheese

½ cup shredded cheddar cheese

1 cup sour cream, for serving

Preheat the oven to 350°F.

Melt the butter in a large skillet over medium heat. Add the onion and sauté until the onion is soft, about 5 minutes. Add the ground beef and cook until it is no longer pink, about 7 minutes. Drain off excess grease. Add the tomato sauce and chilies and simmer for 6 minutes. Remove from the heat.

Beat the eggs and half-and-half together and add to the skillet. Season with salt and pepper to taste.

In a 2-quart casserole, layer the corn chips and pretzels and pour the meat mixture over it. Top with the cheeses.

Bake for 25 minutes, until the cheese bubbles. Serve with sour cream.

Makes 8 to 10 servings

Meat Loaf

MAKES 8 TO 10 SERVINGS

1½ pounds ground beef

½ pound ground pork

1 medium onion, diced

1 green bell pepper, diced

1 tablespoon Worcestershire
sauce

2 teaspoons garlic powder

2 tablespoons ketchup,
plus more as needed

1 cup crushed pretzels

1 egg

Preheat the oven to 375F.

Combine all the ingredients in a large mixing bowl. Place the mixture into a loaf pan or shape it into a loaf shape and place it on a parchment-lined baking sheet with sides or a roasting pan (if you use a roasting pan, you can use a rack to keep the meat loaf out of the grease).

Bake for 30 minutes. Remove from the heat and top with additional ketchup, if desired. Return the meat loaf to the oven to bake for 10 minutes more.

Pretzel-Crusted Catfish

MAKES 4 SERVINGS

1 cup crushed pretzels

¼ cup all-purpose flour

1 teaspoon garlic powder

1 teaspoon dried thyme

4 tablespoons butter, melted

4 (4- to 6-ounce) catfish fillets

Preheat the oven to 350°F.

Combine the pretzels, flour, garlic powder, and thyme in a platter or baking pan. Dip the fish in the butter, and then into the flour mixture. Place on a parchment-lined baking sheet and bake for 15 minutes, until the fish flakes easily with a fork.

Crab Cakes

MAKES 6 TO 8 SERVINGS

1 pound lump crabmeat

¼ pound (1 stick) butter

½ cup minced onion

½ cup minced celery

2 tablespoons minced red or green bell pepper

1 garlic clove, minced

1 egg

¼ cup mayonnaise

2 teaspoons Worcestershire sauce

1 tablespoons Old Bay seasoning

1 cup soft breadcrumbs

1 cup crushed pretzels

Rinse and pick over the crabmeat, being careful to discard any pieces of cartilage or shell.

Melt 4 tablespoons of butter in a large skillet over low heat. Add the onion, celery, bell pepper, and garlic, and gently sauté until tender, about 7 minutes.

Whisk the egg, mayonnaise, Worcestershire sauce, and Old Bay seasoning together in a bowl. Add to the vegetables, along with the breadcrumbs, and pretzels, mixing well. Stir in the crabmeat. Form 6 to 8 loose patties. Place on waxed paper and refrigerate until firm, about 1 hour.

Heat the remaining 4 tablespoons butter in a large skillet over medium-low heat. Put the crab cakes in the skillet and cook for 5 minutes on each side.

Drain on paper towels and serve.

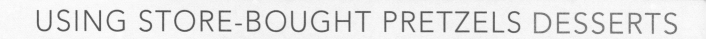

USING STORE-BOUGHT PRETZELS DESSERTS

Pretzel Fondue

MAKES 6 TO 8 SERVINGS

2 cups chocolate chips

3 tablespoons heavy cream

2 teaspoons vanilla extract

1 teaspoon cherry extract

1 (10-ounce) bag pretzel rods

Heat the chocolate chips, cream, and extracts in a saucepan over low heat for 10 minutes, stirring, until the chocolate is completely melted. Transfer to a fondue pot or bowl and serve with the pretzel rods.

Microwave Pretzel Fudge

MAKES ABOUT 24 SQUARES

4 cups confectioners' sugar

¼ pound (1 stick) butter

½ cup cocoa powder

¼ cup milk

2 teaspoons vanilla extract

½ cup crushed pretzels

Combine the confectioners' sugar, butter, cocoa powder, milk and vanilla in a saucepan. Cook over medium heat for 4 minutes, until the mixture is smooth and the ingredients are thoroughly incorporated. Add the pretzels and stir to coat them.

Pour the pretzel mixture out onto a wax-paper-lined baking sheet and refrigerate for 1 hour. Cut into sqaures.

Peanut Butter and Pretzel Fudge

MAKES ABOUT 24 SQUARES

¼ pound (1 stick) butter

2¼ cups brown sugar

½ cup milk

¾ cup creamy peanut butter

2½ teaspoons vanilla extract

3½ cups confectioners' sugar

¾ cup crushed pretzels

Melt the butter in a medium saucepan over medium heat. Stir in the brown sugar and milk. Bring to a boil, and boil for 2 minutes, stirring constantly. Remove from the heat and stir in the peanut butter and vanilla extract.

In a separate bowl, combine the confectioners' sugar with the pretzels. Pour the milk mixture over the pretzels and stir to combine. Pour the mixture into an 8 x 8-inch baking dish and refrigerate for 2 hours, until firm. To serve, cut into squares.

Crunchy Chewy Pretzel Bars

MAKES ABOUT 24 BARS

¼ pound (1 stick) butter, melted

½ cup crushed pretzels

1 cup graham cracker crumbs

1 (14-ounce) can sweetened condensed milk

1½ cups semisweet chocolate chips

1⅓ cups sweetened coconut flakes

1 cup chopped pecans

Preheat the oven to 350°F.

Combine the butter, pretzels, and graham cracker crumbs in a large bowl. Pour the mixture into a 13 x 9-inch baking pan and press to form a crust. Pour the condensed milk over the crust, then spread the chocolate chips, coconut flakes, and pecans over the crust and press down firmly.

Bake for 25 minutes, until lightly browned. Let cool and cut into bars to serve.

Pretzel Congo Bars

MAKES ABOUT 24 BARS

10 tablespoons butter

2⅓ cups brown sugar, packed

3 eggs

2½ cups all-purpose flour

2 teaspoons baking powder

¾ cup chocolate chips

½ cup coconut flakes

½ cup crushed pretzels

½ cup chopped pecans,
  walnuts, or hazelnuts

Preheat the oven to 350°F. Spray a 15 x 10-inch baking pan with nonstick cooking spray.

In a large bowl, cream the butter and brown sugar with an electric mixer on high speed for 5 minutes. Add the eggs, one at a time, blending well after each addition. Stir in the flour and baking powder. Fold in the chocolate chips, coconut flakes, pretzels, and pecans. Pour the mixture into the prepared pan and spread evenly.

Bake for 20 to 25 minutes, until the top is lightly browned. Cool for about 10 minutes before cutting into bars.

Makes about 24 bars

Oatmeal-Butterscotch Pretzel Bars

MAKES ABOUT 24 BARS

2 cups all-purpose flour

2 teaspoons baking powder

1 teaspoon baking soda

½ pound (2 sticks) butter, softened

1½ cups brown sugar, firmly packed

2 eggs

1 tablespoon water

1 cup quick-cooking oats

¾ cup crushed pretzels

2 cups butterscotch chips

½ teaspoon orange extract

1 teaspoon vanilla extract

Preheat the oven to 375°F. Spray the bottom and sides of a 15 x 10-inch baking pan with nonstick cooking spray.

In a small bowl, combine the flour, baking powder, and baking soda.

In a large bowl, cream the butter and brown sugar with an electric mixer on medium speed. Add the eggs one at a time, mixing thoroughly after each addition. Stir in the water. Beat until creamy. Add the flour mixture, ¼ cup at a time, until thoroughly incorporated. Stir in the oats, pretzels, butterscotch chips, and extracts. Spread the mixture into the prepared baking pan.

Bake for 20 to 25 minutes. Cool to room temperature before cutting into squares.

Pretzel Lemon Squares

MAKES ABOUT 24 SQUARES

½ cup crushed pretzels

1½ cups graham cracker crumbs

7 tablespoons butter, melted

2 tablespoons sugar

5 eggs

6 tablespoons all-purpose flour

½ cup lemon juice

⅓ cup confectioners' sugar, plus
   more for garnish

Preheat the oven to 350°F. Spray a 13 x 9-inch baking pan with non-stick cooking spray.

Combine the pretzels, graham cracker crumbs, butter, and sugar in a bowl. Press the mixture into the prepared pan.

Bake for 20 minutes.

Meanwhile, beat the eggs, flour, lemon juice, and confectioners' sugar with an electric mixer on low speed for 3 to 5 minutes, until the mixture is smooth. Pour over the hot crust.

Bake for 25 minutes, until the top is golden brown. Cool to room temperature, dust with the confectioners' sugar, and cut into squares.

Chocolate-Dipped Pretzels

MAKES 12 DIPPED PRETZELS

4 ounces chocolate candy
  coating (almond bark)
  (see note on page 127)

12 pretzel rods

1 cup mini chocolate chips

Microwave the candy coating in a microwave-safe bowl for 30 seconds. Dip half of each pretzel in the candy coating. Roll in the chocolate chips and place on wax paper to cool.

Chocolate Marshmallow Dipped Pretzels

MAKES 12 DIPPED PRETZELS

1 cup marshmallow cream

4 ounces chocolate candy
  coating (almond bark)
  (see note on page 127)

12 pretzel rods

1 cup semisweet chocolate
  chips

Microwave the marshmallow cream in a microwave-safe bowl on medium power for 15 to 20 seconds, until it has melted and is easy to work with.

Microwave the candy coating for 30 seconds, until it melts.

Dip half of each pretzel in the marshmallow cream, then in the candy coating. Roll the pretzels in the chocolate chips and place on wax paper to set.

Margarita Cheesecake

MAKES A 9-INCH CHEESE-
CAKE, SERVES 8 TO 10

CRUST

1 cup crushed pretzels

⅓ cup sugar

5 tablespoons butter, melted

FILLING

3 (8-ounce) packages cream
cheese, softened

¾ cup sugar

4 eggs

1 cup sour cream

2 tablespoons golden tequila

2 tablespoons orange juice

1 tablespoon grated lime zest

Preheat the oven to 325°F. Place the top oven rack in the center of the oven. Butter the bottom and sides of a 9½-inch springform pan. Place the pan on top of a sheet of foil and wrap the foil around the bottom of the pan.

To make the crust, process the pretzels in a food processor until they are fine crumbs. Add the sugar and butter. Process until well combined. Press the pretzel mixture into the bottom and partially up the sides of the prepared pan. Refrigerate.

To make the filling, combine the cream cheese and sugar in a large bowl, and beat with an electric mixer on medium speed for 2 minutes, until the mixture becomes light and creamy. Add the eggs, one at a time, beating well after each addition. Scrape down the sides of the bowl as you go. Add the sour cream, tequila, orange juice, and lime zest. The mixture should be smooth.

Pour the mixture into the crust. Place the springform pan in a large roasting pan and carefully fill the roasting pan with boiling water so that it comes about halfway up the sides of the springform pan.

Bake the cheesecake for 45 minutes to 1 hour, until the center is set. Let the cheesecake cool to room temperature on a rack. Refrigerate for 2 hours before serving.

Chocolate-Orange Cheesecake

MAKES A 9-INCH CHEESE-
CAKE, SERVES 8 TO 10

CRUST

1 cup chocolate cook crumbs

½ cup crushed pretzels

3 tablespoons butter, melted

¼ cup sugar

FILLING

1 cup sugar

3 (8-ounce) packages
cream cheese, softened

5 eggs

2 tablespoons orange juice or
Grand Marnier

½ teaspoon grated orange zest

4 ounces chocolate chips

Preheat the oven to 325°F. Place the top oven rack in the center of the oven. Butter the bottom and sides of a 9½-inch springform pan.

To make the crust, combine the cookie crumbs, pretzels, butter, and sugar in a bowl and mix well . Press the mixture into the bottom of the prepared pan. Bake the crust for 10 minutes; set aside to cool.

To make the filling, cream the sugar and cream cheese with an electric mixer on medium speed until smooth. Beat in the eggs, one at a time. Gradually stir in the orange juice and zest. Pour half the batter into the prepared crust and refrigerate.

Microwave the chocolate chips in a microwave-safe bowl for 45 seconds. Stir until the chocolate is thoroughly melted. Let the chocolate cool slightly, then add it to the remaining filling, stirring well to incorporate.

Spoon the chocolate filling over the chilled layer of filling. Use a knife to make a swirling design in the fillings.

Bake the cheesecake for 1 hour, until the center is almost set. Cool to room temperature, then refrigerate for 3 hours, until the cheese-cake sets.

Lemon Cream Cheese Pie

MAKES A 9-INCH PIE,
SERVES 8 TO 10

CRUST

1 cup graham cracker crumbs

½ cup crushed pretzels

3 tablespoons sugar

5 tablespoons butter, melted

FILLING

¼ cup sugar

8 ounces cream cheese, softened

3 eggs

½ cup corn syrup

2 teaspoons grated lemon zest

⅓ cup lemon juice

1 tablespoon cornstarch

2 tablespoons butter, melted

Whipped cream, for garnish

Preheat the oven to 350°F.

To make the pie crust, combine the graham cracker crumbs, crushed pretzels, sugar, and butter. Press into a 9-inch pie pan.

To make the filling, cream the remaining sugar and cream cheese with an electric mixer until smooth and creamy, about 5 minutes. Add 1 egg and mix well.

Pour the filling into the pie crust and spread evenly. Refrigerate while you continue with the recipe.

In a large bowl, combine the remaining 2 eggs, with the corn syrup, lemon zest, lemon juice, cornstarch, and butter. Mix with an electric mixer on medium for 6 minutes, until smooth. Pour over the chilled filling.

Bake the pie for 50 to 55 minutes, until the filling is set and the crust is golden. Cool on a rack before serving. Garnish with whipped cream.

Key Lime Pie

MAKES A 9-INCH PIE,
SERVES 8 TO 10

CRUST

1 cup graham cracker crumbs

½ cup crushed pretzels

6 tablespoons unsalted butter, melted

¼ cup sugar

FILLING

4 egg yolks

¼ cup grated lime zest

1 (14-ounce) can sweetened condensed milk

½ cup lime juice

Preheat the oven to 325°F.

To make the crust, combine the graham cracker crumbs, pretzels, butter, and sugar in a bowl and stir with a fork until well blended. Pour the crumb mixture into a 9-inch pie pan and press into the bottom and sides.

Bake for 15 minutes, until the crust is light brown. Cool to room temperature.

To make the filling, combine the egg yolks and lime zest in a bowl and whisk for 2 minutes, until the mixture is thoroughly mixed and light green. Beat in the condensed milk, then the lime juice. Set the mixture aside at room temperature for 30 minutes, until it thickens.

When the filling is thick and the crust is cool, pour the filling into the crust. Bake the pie for 15 minutes, until the filling is somewhat set, but stills jiggles when shaken. Cool to room temperature, then refrigerate for 4 hours, until the filling is set.

Pumpkin Pie with Pretzel Topping

MAKES A 9-INCH PIE,
SERVES 8 TO 10

1 teaspoon all-purpose flour

¾ cup sugar

½ teaspoon ground ginger

2 teaspoons ground cinnamon

½ cup molasses

1¼ cups pumpkin purée

2 eggs, lightly beaten

1 teaspoon vanilla extract

1 cup evaporated milk

2 tablespoons water

1 unbaked 9-inch piecrust

3 tablespoons butter

½ cup chopped pecans

¼ cup crushed pretzels

¼ teaspoon nutmeg

Preheat the oven to 375°F.

In a medium-sized mixing bowl, combine the flour, ½ cup of the sugar, ginger, 1½ teaspoons of the cinnamon, molasses, pumpkin, and eggs and stir well. Add the vanilla, evaporated milk, and water, mixing well to incorporate. Pour into the prepared piecrust and refrigerate.

Melt the butter in a saucepan over medium heat, then add the remaining ¼ cup sugar and stir to combine. Add the pecans, pretzels, the remaining ½ teaspoon cinnamon, and the nutmeg and stir well. Cook for 5 minutes, until a thick syrup forms. Pour the syrup over the pie.

Bake the pie for 40 minutes, until center is set. Let the pie cool to room temperature on a rack.

Peanut Butter and Banana Pie

- -

MAKES A 9-INCH PIE,
SERVES 8 TO 10

CRUST

3 tablespoons butter

1 cup graham cracker crumbs

⅓ cup crushed pretzels

¼ cup sugar

¼ cup unsalted peanuts, minced

Chopped peanuts, for garnish

FILLING

18 large marshmallows

½ cup milk

1 teaspoon vanilla extract

½ cup creamy peanut butter

2 cups whipped topping or
    whipped cream

3 medium bananas, sliced

Preheat the oven to 375°F.

To make the crust, stir together the butter, graham cracker crumbs, pretzels, sugar, and peanuts. Press the mixture into a 9-inch pie plate. Bake for 7 minutes. Cool and set aside.

To make the filling, heat the marshmallows and milk in a heavy saucepan over medium heat. Stir constantly until the marshmallows melt completely, then stir in the vanilla. Remove from the heat and stir in the peanut butter. Cool to room temperature, then fold in the whipped topping.

Arrange 2 of the bananas on the bottom of the crust, then spoon the filling over them. Garnish with the remaining banana slices and the peanuts. Refrigerate for 2 hours, until the filling sets.

Lazy Banana Cream Pretzel Pie

MAKES A 9-INCH PIE,
SERVES 8 TO 10

CRUST

1 cup crushed pretzels

½ cup graham cracker crumbs

1 tablespoon sugar

4 tablespoons butter, melted

FILLING

1 to 2 bananas, sliced

¼ cup confectioners' sugar

1 cup heavy cream

2 cups cold milk

2 (0.8-ounce) packages instant
   banana cream pudding mix

Caramel Pretzel Dip, for serving
   (page 168)

To make the crust, combine the pretzels, graham cracker crumbs, sugar, and butter in a bowl. Press into a 9-inch pie pan.

Arrange the banana slices to cover the pie crust. Refrigerate while you continue with the filling.

To make the filling, beat the confectioners' sugar and cream with an electric mixer on high for 5 minutes, until stiff peaks form. Set aside.

In a large bowl, combine the milk and pudding mix. Beat with a wire whisk for 2 minutes, until well blended. Gently fold in one-third of the whipped cream. Spoon this mixture into the crust. Top with the remaining whipped cream and refrigerate for 4 hours or until set.

Drizzle with Caramel Sauce before serving.

Ice Cream Pie with Pretzel Crust

MAKES A 9-INCH PIE,
SERVES 8 TO 10

1½ cups crushed pretzels

5 tablespoons butter, melted

2 tablespoons sugar

3½ cups ice cream, your choice
of flavor

½ cup chocolate sprinkles

Preheat the oven to 300°F.

To make the crust, combine the pretzels, butter, and sugar in a large bowl. Press into a 9-inch glass pie dish and bake for 7 minutes. Set aside to cool.

Spoon the ice cream into the pie crust and smooth. Sprinkle with chocolate sprinkles. Cover with plastic wrap and freeze until ready to serve.

Eggnog Pretzel Pie

MAKES A 9-INCH PIE,
SERVES 8 TO 10

¾ cups crushed pretzels

3 tablespoons sugar

4 tablespoons butter, melted

1 (1.5-ounce) package instant
vanilla pudding

3 cups milk

2 teaspoons rum extract

1 teaspoon brandy extract

½ teaspoon cinnamon

½ teaspoon nutmeg

2 cups whipped cream

To make the crust, combine the pretzels, sugar, and butter in a bowl. Press the mixture into a 9-inch pie pan.

To make the filling, combine the pudding mix, milk, extracts, cinnamon, and nutmeg, and beat with an electric mixer for 2 minutes. Fold in 1 cup of the whipped cream and pour the mixture into the prepared pie crust. Refrigerate for 2 hours or until set.

Top with remaining whipped cream.

PRETZELICIOUS DIPPING SAUCES

Honey Butter Pretzel Dip

- -

MAKES ABOUT 1½ CUPS

½ pound (2 sticks) butter

½ cup honey

Minced fresh parsley, for garnish

Melt the butter in a heavy saucepan over medium-low heat. Whisk in the honey.

Herb Butter Pretzel Dip

- -

MAKES ABOUT 1 CUP

½ pound (2 sticks) butter

½ teaspoon dried marjoram

½ teaspoon dried thyme

½ teaspoon dried tarragon

1 teaspoon minced fresh parsley

Melt the butter in a saucepan over low heat for 5 minutes. Add the herbs and stir well.

Honey Mustard Pretzel Dip

MAKES ABOUT 1½ CUPS

1 cup mustard

½ cup honey

½ teaspoon ground mustard

Combine all of the ingredients in a small bowl and whisk until thoroughly mixed.

Herb-Mustard Pretzel Dip

MAKES ABOUT 1½ CUPS

1 cup Dijon mustard

¼ cup white wine

2 tablespoons freshly minced herbs, such as rosemary, thyme, marjoram, chives

Combine all the ingredients in a small bowl and whisk until thoroughly mixed.

Garlic-Butter Pretzel Dip

MAKES ABOUT 1½ CUPS

½ pound (2 sticks) butter

2 garlic cloves, minced

2 tablespoons minced fresh
  parsley

In a medium saucepan over low heat, combine the butter and garlic and stir until the butter melts and the garlic is soft, about 6 minutes. Remove from the heat and add the parsley.

Blue Cheese Pretzel Dip

MAKES ABOUT 2 CUPS

¼ pound crumbled blue cheese

½ cup mayonnaise

½ cup sour cream

1 tablespoon champagne
  vinegar

1 teaspoon lemon juice

Pinch white pepper

Combine all of the ingredients in a small bowl and whisk until thoroughly mixed.

Alfredo Pretzel Dip

MAKES ABOUT 4 CUPS

¼ pound (1 stick) butter

1 pint heavy cream

2 tablespoons cream cheese

¾ cup grated Parmesan cheese

1½ teaspoons garlic powder

¼ teaspoon nutmeg

Melt the butter in a medium saucepan over medium heat. Add the remaining ingredients and cook for 7 minutes, until the mixture bubbles slightly and is smooth and creamy.

Auntie's Raita Pretzel Dip

MAKES ABOUT 4 CUPS

2 cups Greek yogurt

1 small red onion, minced

1 tomato, seeded and finely diced

½ cup seeded and minced cucumber

1 tablespoon minced coriander leaves

½ teaspoon coarsely ground cumin seeds, toasted

Salt

Combine all the ingredients in a large bowl and refrigerate until ready to serve.

Marinara Pretzel Dip

MAKES ABOUT 6 CUPS

½ cup extra-virgin olive oil

½ cup minced onions

¼ cup minced garlic

1 teaspoon salt

½ teaspoon pepper

2 teaspoons dried oregano

1 tablespoon dried basil

1 (28-ounce) can plum tomatoes

1 (28-ounce) can puréed tomatoes

2 tablespoons red wine

1 teaspoon sugar

Heat the oil in a large, heavy saucepan over medium heat. Add the garlic and onions and sauté for 5 minutes, until the onions are translucent. Add the salt, pepper, oregano, basil, tomatoes, wine, and sugar and simmer over medium-low heat for 15 minutes.

Eggplant Pretzel Dip

- -

MAKES ABOUT 4 CUPS

1 large eggplant

Kosher salt

1 red onion, diced

1 red bell pepper, diced

3 garlic cloves

3 tablespoons extra-virgin
  olive oil

1 teaspoon dried thyme

1 teaspoon marjoram

½ cup prepared hummus

Juice of 1 lemon

Salt and pepper

Peel and dice the eggplant and place in a colander that is set over a bowl. Sprinkle the eggplant with salt. Set aside for 1 hour.

Rinse the eggplant thoroughly and pat dry.

Preheat the oven to 350°F.

Place the eggplant, onion, and garlic on a baking sheet and drizzle with the olive oil. Sprinkle the thyme and marjoram over the vegetables and toss to coat.

Bake for 15 minutes, until the vegetables are soft.

Transfer the vegetables to the bowl of a food processor and pulse until a smooth paste forms. Spoon the vegetable mixture into a bowl and add the hummus and lemon juice. Season with salt and pepper to taste and stir to combine.

Hoisin Pretzel Dip

MAKES ABOUT 2 CUPS

1 cup prepared hoisin sauce

½ cup light soy sauce

1 teaspoon grated fresh ginger

1 teaspoon red bell pepper flakes

2 teaspoons sesame oil

2 tablespoons rice wine vinegar

2 minced green onions

Combine all the ingredients in a small bowl and whisk until thoroughly mixed.

Martini Pretzel Dip

MAKES ABOUT 1 CUP

¾ cup mayonnaise

¼ cup sour cream

2 tablespoons minced shallots

2 tablespoons minced cocktail olives

½ teaspoon dried thyme

3 tablespoons extra-dry vermouth

Combine all the ingredients in a small bowl and whisk until thoroughly mixed.

Yummy Yogurt Pretzel Dip

MAKES ABOUT 3 CUPS

2 cups nonfat vanilla yogurt

2 teaspoons vanilla extract

½ cup crushed pineapple,
  drained

1 teaspoon minced fresh mint

Combine all the ingredients in a small bowl and stir until thoroughly mixed.

Caramel Pretzel Dip

MAKES ABOUT 4 CUPS

2 cups light brown sugar

14 ounces sweetened
  condensed milk

¼ pound (1 stick) butter

2 teaspoons vanilla extract

½ cup whole milk

Combine the brown sugar and condensed milk in a heavy saucepan over medium low heat, and stir for 5 to 7 minutes, until the sugar dissolves.

Remove from the heat and add the butter, vanilla, and milk. Store in the refrigerator until ready to use.

CONVERSION CHARTS

FORMULAS FOR METRIC CONVERSION

Ounces to grams	multiply ounces by 28.35
Pounds to grams	multiply pounds by 453.5
Cups to liters	multiply cups by .24
Fahrenheit to Centigrade	subtract 32 from Fahrenheit, multiply by five and divide by 9

METRIC EQUIVALENTS FOR VOLUME

U.S.		Metric
⅛ tsp.		0.6 ml
½ tsp.		2.5 ml
¾ tsp.		4.0 ml
1 tsp.		5.0 ml
1½ tsp.		7.0 ml
2 tsp.		10.0 ml
3 tsp.		15.0 ml
4 tsp.		20.0 ml
1 Tbsp.	—	15.0 ml
1½ Tbsp.	—	22.0 ml
2 Tbsp. (⅛ cup)	1 fl. oz	30.0 ml
2½ Tbsp.	—	37.0 ml
3 Tbsp.	—	44.0 ml
⅓ cup	—	57.0 ml
4 Tbsp. (¼ cup)	2 fl. oz	59.0 ml
5 Tbsp.	—	74.0 ml
6 Tbsp.	—	89.0 ml
8 Tbsp. (½ cup)	4 fl. oz	120.0 ml
¾ cup	6 fl. oz	178.0 ml
1 cup	8 fl. oz	237.0 ml (.24 liters)
1½ cups	—	354.0 ml
1¾ cups	—	414.0 ml
2 cups (1 pint)	16 fl. oz	473.0 ml
4 cups (1 quart)	32 fl. oz	(.95 liters)
5 cups	—	(1.183 liters)
16 cups (1 gallon)	128 fl. oz	(3.8 liters)

OVEN TEMPERATURES

Degrees Fahrenheit	Degrees Centigrade	British Gas Marks
200°	93°	—
250°	120°	—
275°	140°	1
300°	150°	2
325°	165°	3
350°	175°	4
375°	190°	5
400°	200°	6
450°	230°	8

METRIC EQUIVALENTS FOR BUTTER

U.S.	Metric
2 tsp.	10.0 g
1 Tbsp.	15.0 g
1½ Tbsp.	22.5 g
2 Tbsp. (1 oz)	55.0 g
3 Tbsp.	70.0 g
¼ lb. (1 stick)	110.0 g
½ lb. (2 sticks)	220.0 g

METRIC EQUIVALENTS FOR LENGTH

U.S.	Metric
¼ inch	.65 cm
½ inch	1.25 cm
1 inch	2.50 cm
2 inches	5.00 cm
3 inches	6.00 cm
4 inches	8.00 cm
5 inches	11.00 cm
6 inches	15.00 cm
7 inches	18.00 cm
8 inches	20.00 cm
9 inches	23.00 cm
12 inches	30.50 cm
15 inches	38.00 cm

METRIC EQUIVALENTS FOR WEIGHT

U.S.	Metric
1 oz	28 g
2 oz	58 g
3 oz	85 g
4 oz (¼ lb.)	113 g
5 oz	142 g
6 oz	170 g
7 oz	199 g
8 oz (½ lb.)	227 g
10 oz	284 g
12 oz (¾ lb.)	340 g
14 oz	397 g
16 oz (1 lb.)	454 g

INDEX